Memorial
BOOK
COLLECTION

FRANK A. MILLER

IN RECOGNITION OF HIS
CONSTANT LABOR IN THE
PROMOTION OF CIVIC BEAUTY
COMMUNITY RIGHTEOUSNESS
AND WORLD PEACE

influential styles

JUDITH MILLER   photography by Simon Upton

influential styles

**FROM BAROQUE TO BAUHAUS –
INSPIRATION FOR TODAY'S INTERIORS**

Watson-Guptill Publications / New York

First published in the United States in 2003
by Watson-Guptill Publications
a division of VNU Business Media, Inc.
770 Broadway, New York, New York 10003
www.watsonguptill.com

Conceived and produced by Jacqui Small
an imprint of Aurum Press Limited
25 Bedford Avenue
London WC1B 3AT

Publisher: Jacqui Small
Editorial manager: Vicki Vrint
Design: Maggie Town, Beverly Price
Project editor: Catherine Rubinstein
Chief contributor: Jill Bace
Location researcher: Nadine Bazar
Production: Geoff Barlow

Library of Congress Control Number:
2003105410
ISBN: 0-8230-2527-6

Manufactured in China

1 2 3 4 5 6 7 / 07 06 05 04 03 02 03

contents

INTRODUCTION

Throughout the centuries, there have been a number of decorative styles that have endured in interior design, emerging again and again and always reinterpreted in fresh and exciting ways. These styles, along with their national as well as regional variations, have continuously presented an extensive assortment of highly creative and inspirational ideas in the fields of architecture, interior decoration, and ornament.

Styles in interior design tend to be cyclical. What was influential in the past can be influential today. But not all of these stylistic movements of the past are at home in the modern interior. This book focuses on several of the most enduring and important of these styles—styles that reemerge with every generation—and illustrates how they have been adapted for today. These inspirational styles include the aesthetically appealing symmetry and proportion of the classical, the simplicity and natural warmth of country, which celebrates rural charms, the highly individual decorative tradition that draws inspiration from cultures around the world, and the

revolutionary modern styles of the twentieth century. Looking at the timeless appeal of these very different approaches to interior decoration within their historical context, it becomes clear how what came before remains relevant to modern life.

Perhaps no other style has had greater impact on the history of design than the classical. Since the Italian Renaissance in the fourteenth century, the architectural traditions of ancient Greece and Rome have exercised enormous influence on the art and design of subsequent cultures, providing a vocabulary of ornament that has been almost constantly revived and reinterpreted to the present day. This classical revival was inspired initially by archaeological excavations of the architecture and artifacts that had survived from ancient Rome. The rediscovered Greco-Roman architectural principles and devices such as temple-front porticoes, pediments, and rusticated masonry were adopted not only for architectural ornament, but also for furniture, textiles, and decorative objects, including vases and urns.

By the sixteenth century, Renaissance architecture and ornament had begun to diverge into two related but distinct styles. The classicism championed by architects such as Andrea Palladio endeavored to preserve the integrity and purity of original Roman forms, while architects such as Michelangelo and Giulio Romano expanded upon classical Roman forms such as columns and brackets in a sculptural fashion, frequently ignoring their original structural function by employing them purely for visual impact.

The elegance, serenity, and harmony of proportion promoted by Palladio formed the cornerstone of a classical revival in England during the early eighteenth century. Popular in North America, the bold, austere Palladian style boasted impressive architectural elements, such as temple-front porticoes, coffered ceilings, and rusticated masonry, although it ultimately came to rely on the harmony of proportion and detail for decorative effect.

The second half of the eighteenth century witnessed another revitalization of antique inspiration. In part inspired by archaeological discoveries in southern Italy, and championed by the Scottish architect Robert Adam, this influential neoclassical style was widely adopted on both sides of the Atlantic—from the Gustavian strand of Scandinavia to the Federal style that emerged in the United States. Luxurious, opulent versions of the neoclassical—the French Empire and English Regency styles—not only looked to Rome, but also drew from a lexicon of decorative ornament derived from ancient Greek, Etruscan, and Egyptian antiquity.

FAR LEFT This 1843 Greek Revival church in Catskill, New York, embodies the elements of Hudson River architecture of the period: the white-painted clapboards and classical Corinthian columns.

LEFT A New England-style saltbox house built in the 1730s, with an attic added in the 1750s, has weathered clapboards originally used on boats transporting ice to New York City. The roof has original cedar shakes.

ABOVE LEFT Mustio Manor (or Svarta Manor in Swedish) was built between 1783 and 1792 in classical Gustavian style. Although it is in Finland, the styling and architecture is Swedish.

ABOVE Symmetry above all else is the essence of classicism. Everything in this symmetrical courtyard garden leads to the pavilion beyond.

Throughout the nineteenth century, classicism retained a hold on the imagination on both sides of the Atlantic. From the mid-1920s, however, it was supplanted by the Art Deco taste, and by the minimalist Modern movement led by architects and designers such as Le Corbusier, Walter Gropius, and Ludwig Mies van der Rohe.

In the second half of the twentieth century, Post-modern architects and designers, rejecting the relentless rationality of the minimalists, "rediscovered" classicism. With bravado they took unornamented Modernist interiors and embellished them with fabrics, furniture, artifacts, and fixtures that were either directly modeled on or inspired by classical originals. Today the contemporary interior—with clean, spare lines and sparse ornament harking back to minimalism—marries effectively with the simplicity and harmonious proportions of the architectural designs of classical antiquity and their related objects.

Alongside the classical, another decorative style that has consistently been inspirational in interior design is that derived from the rural past. The universal appeal of country style—comfortable and unselfconscious—lies in a tradition of simplicity and a natural approach to living. Having evolved out of necessity, as the rural poor created interiors and furnishings that were at once commodious and long lasting, country style offers an attractive alternative to structured, formal approaches. Decorative yet functional, it celebrates the virtues of craftsmanship. Today the timeless charms of country style, both grand and rustic, symbolize an ideal way of life and offer a pleasing sanctuary from the pressures of modern living.

ABOVE This seventeenth- and eighteenth-century chartreuse, a hunting or country lodge, in the Périgord region of southwestern France, has the mellow stone and roof lines typical of the area.

ABOVE RIGHT A space-age folly lands in rural Normandy. This three-story concrete house was built in 1973–76 by a wealthy contractor's son, who had spent several months living in San Francisco.

RIGHT The Danes love colors and have for centuries used a variety of naturally occurring pigments to adorn both the interiors and exteriors of their homes, as here on the island of Funen.

FAR RIGHT In Post-modernist architecture one of the main themes is simplicity. In this house, designed by John Pawson, the outside mirrors the interior in form, structure, and materials.

LEFT In this apartment in Munich, the classicism is reflected in works of art. The painting in the forefront is by the symbolist painter Sascha Schneider. Titled "His Fate," it was painted in Dresden in 1894. It was intended to portray the end of the old order and old way of ruling, represented by church and monarch being slain, by the new order, representing force and the anonymous state. The eye is then led through to the magnificent bronze "Javelin Thrower" by Karl Mobius, c.1900, which again represents the old order of classicism.

LEFT, BELOW A plywood laminate daybed designed in 1925 covered with a sheepskin, a table, and a lamp from the Gropius House are redolent of the culture of early-twentieth-century Europe, in particular the Bauhaus, of which Walter Gropius was founder and director.

RIGHT Houses are often restyled to keep up with fashion; it is a very recent phenomenon to try to preserve houses in one period style. Although the architectural features of the main hallway in this eighteenth-century manor house in the Dordogne region of southwestern France have remained constant, the decoration was done by itinerant painters, working between 1876 and 1911. At the time, they still used limewash applied in the fresco manner (on wet plaster).

Throughout history, the desire for warmth and comfort has looked to decoration to create a cohesive spirit in an interior while articulating individual style and personal taste. Decorative schemes that rely on various cross-cultural currents and ornamental traditions inevitably evoke the sensuous and exotic influences of cultures from across the globe. From colorful painted walls embracing ancient folk traditions to the sumptuous exoticism of Africa or the Orient, this provides a fertile vocabulary for artistic expression.

Interiors of the twenty-first century rejoice in the past, looking to a variety of sources for inspiration to create a unique and individual style, be it classical or country, decorative or modern. An amalgam of patterns and colors—bold and vibrant, pale and delicate, whether looking back to eighteenth-century interpretations of the classical or the colorful and spirited vision of the 1960s: at the heart of today's interiors is the inspiration of times past. These interiors breathe the best from the traditions that have gone before, while exulting in the possibilities of the present and the future.

NEOCLASSICAL

FROM THE MID-EIGHTEENTH century onward, a renewed appreciation of classical tradition, fueled by archaeological discoveries at Herculaneum and Pompeii in Italy, found architects and designers looking to the ancient world for inspiration. In part a reaction to the flamboyance of Rococo, a style developed that was at once dignified and restrained, adopting the pleasing symmetry, proportion, and purity of form inherent in the architecture, ornament, furnishings, and artifacts of ancient Greece and Rome. Buildings emulated their architecture, and the rich vocabulary of classical ornament—including rosettes, acanthus leaves, garlands, and palmettes—was used in interiors. Antique vases and urns lent forms to a host of household objects in silver, glass, ceramics, and bronze. By the 1770s, most of Europe had embraced the elegant neoclassical style, which remained influential on both sides of the Atlantic well into the nineteenth century and beyond.

The Scottish architect Robert Adam was largely responsible for developing early neoclassicism, especially in Britain. His style was eclectic, combining what he saw in the buildings of ancient Rome and Pompeii, the engravings of the Italian architect Piranesi, and Italian Renaissance houses. These ideas he added to a large repertoire of decorative elements derived from ancient Greek and Etruscan ornamentation.

EARLY NEOCLASSICAL

Adam's style conceived a building as a coordinated whole, harmonizing the exterior with the interior and decorative objects. Mathematical neoclassical spirit echoes in the straight lines and delicate proportions of Adam's furniture designs, while the forms of his coffee urns, vases, and tureens are inspired by classical equivalents. His many ornamental motifs— guilloches, swags and festoons, griffins, laurel leaves and anthemia, medallions, and palmettes—are drawn from the classical lexicon.

The Adam style spread throughout Europe, chiefly via pattern books, and achieved high popularity in Italy, Germany, Russia, and France. In the latter, during the reign of Louis XVI, it was much admired for its elegance, and was enthusiastically endorsed by architects and designers, who used opulent materials while maintaining classical restraint. Neoclassicism spread to America as well, where it formed the basis of early Federal style.

An important strand of the style is found in Scandinavia. Known as Gustavian, it takes its name from the Swedish monarch Gustav III, under whom French neoclassicism was adapted into a uniquely Scandinavian version, characterized by restrained classical proportions and clean lines, but with less rich materials and a lighter color palette than in France.

In the United States, the main phase of neoclassicism, c.1780–1820, known as Federal style, is characterized by slender proportions, flat surfaces, thin moldings, and delicate ornament. American neoclassicism tended to depend upon the preferences of individual designers. French influence was strong in Philadelphia, for example, while towns such as Baltimore favored the English Adam style.

Light and elegant, Adam style was admired for its architectural grandeur, the subtlety of its distinctive decorative motifs, and the way it integrated architecture and interior.

OPPOSITE: TOP LEFT Grisaille panels with swags of densely packed laurel leaves looped through rams' heads (aegricanes) are common devices that point to an eighteenth-century classical tradition. These were typically used by Robert Adam and also in grand Gustavian decorations.

TOP RIGHT The love of the classical spread throughout Europe and the Americas in the late eighteenth and early nineteenth centuries. This Swedish Empire clock and candlestick could have been made in Paris, London, or Charleston.

BOTTOM LEFT Peter Hone collects classical objects from all periods. An eighteenth-century urn from Enville Hall, Shropshire, England, with its finely carved acanthus leaves, festoons, and garlands of flowers, sits beside a plaster bust, medallions, and a small plaster figure of Apollo.

BOTTOM RIGHT Much neoclassical decoration is not what it seems. Here the stone blocking on the walls is an elaborate paint effect, set off by the plaster portrait medallion.

RIGHT, ABOVE In the grand salon of this Gustavian manor, the dentils along the molding hark back to Roman and Greek architecture. During the eighteenth century, dentils appeared on almost every classical building, in wood, stone, or plaster. The other features, such as the pilasters, architraves, ribbon, and festoons, are trompe l'oeil.

RIGHT And BELOW A combination of real architectural details and painted ones was part of the drama of the "Grand Salon." The high quality of work can be seen in the three-dimensional figure painting in the niche. An elaborate overmantel with a mirror conceals a stove. The fleur-de-lis and coronet are part of the coat of arms of the Linder family, owners of Mustio Manor for over 200 years.

ARCHITECTURE

Symmetry, order, and harmony of proportion and detail are hallmarks of the neoclassical interior. Wall paneling—often with classical columns and pilasters—was widely used, and ceilings tended to be segmented and embellished with shallow plaster moldings, painted decoration, or both. Although Adam favored festoons and garlands, much classical imagery—acanthus and laurel leaves, medallions, rams' heads, sphinxes, urns, and arabesques—was adopted for moldings.

The most prestigious types of flooring were multicolored stone flags or tiles, mosaics, hardwood marquetry and parquetry, and exotically veined marbles. Less-expensive alternatives included boards of polished oak, fir, or pine, sometimes painted to resemble marble or covered with floorcloths, rugs, or woven matting. On occasion, geometrically patterned fitted carpets were installed in the grandest rooms of an Adam interior.

Doors were generally framed and paneled, commonly with six rectangular or square panels. While the grandest were made of polished hardwoods such as mahogany and rosewood, or inlaid with exotic woods including ebony, cherry, and holly, softwood doors were more common. These were painted or grained, with panels and moldings picked out in contrasting colors or gilding. Door surrounds were often based on the five orders of classical architecture: Doric, Ionic, Corinthian, Composite, and Tuscan.

Fireplaces and chimneypieces were made of porphyry, veined marble, sandstone, granite, slate, scagliola, hardwoods, or pine painted to resemble marble. They boasted jambs in the form of columns, pilasters, or caryatids; friezes ornamented with medallions, rosettes, swags, or scrolling foliage; mantel shelves edged with moldings; and sculptural overmantels incorporating mirrors or paintings.

ABOVE As a style, Gustavian is reasonably easy to adapt to a more modern setting. The neoclassical stove is designed to look like a column. The paneled effect on the walls is set against a vast expanse of off-white, with simple garlands of flowers. These designs were straight out of contemporary pattern books of 1780–1785. The mirror is a twentieth-century reproduction of a late-eighteenth-century example. The chair is a simple late-eighteenth-century piece.

ABOVE RIGHT The trompe l'oeil murals in this grand hall were painted by the famous Swedish architect Erik Palmstedt. All trompe l'oeil decorations were painted on canvas. These tones of gray immediately give a Gustavian feel.

RIGHT This Marieburg stove was imported from Sweden to Mustio Manor in Finland. The off-whites, pale and rose pink, and pale blue with a hint of gilding, are typical Gustavian colors. When this room was redecorated, it was found that the original colors were shades of green, also typical of the style.

COLOR AND PATTERN

By the middle of the eighteenth century, the light color palette, with roots in the white-and-gilt reception rooms of late-seventeenth-century French palaces, was taken up for classical interiors by households across Europe and America. Archaeological excavations at Pompeii and Herculaneum in Italy introduced a fashion for colors found there—lilacs, blues, greens, pinks, and black. Some of the paler colors were adopted by Robert Adam for walls and doors—pinks, greens, blues, and muted golds—and frequently lightened by delicate white plasterwork. In addition to white, light

LEFT The stove in this Etruscan-inspired room is an interesting marriage of Gustavian and Rococo styles, again made by Marieburg. Etruscan-style decoration was made popular by archaeological digs at Pompeii and Herculaneum in the mid-eighteenth century. These decorations emulate those at Pompeii, with delicate circular and lozenge-shaped medallions, tripods, urns, leaves, birds, and half-figures often suspended from festoons and husks. The original style was dominated by red, black, and white, but as it inspired decorators such as Robert Adam the colors were tempered by a lighter palette of pale blues, greens, and grays.

LEFT These "Roman murals" were probably painted by Jean-Louis Despres and his student, Pehn Sundberg. Despres had been persuaded to come to Sweden by King Gustav III when he saw his work in Italy in 1784. These quality murals were of high status and showed that the owner of the house was well acquainted with the classics.

RIGHT AND BELOW The subtle interplay of colors and motifs has increased the popularity of the Gustavian style today. Scrolling foliate forms with a grapevine quality are imposed on rose pink to form a panel around a paler pink. There are also shades of gray and blue, off-white, and gilding.

RIGHT In the Gustavian style, motif, pattern, color, and trompe l'oeil are combined to give evidence of the neoclassical. The muted colors and shades of gray and off-white are often in evidence, enlivened by the use of stronger colors—deep blue, rose pink, strong red, gilding, and even black. It is the controlled use of the strong colors and overall sense of restraint that give this style its enduring popularity.

colors included pearl gray and various shades of gold, from straw and pale citron to bright Chinese yellow. More vibrant alternatives— violet, pea green, turquoise, cerise, scarlet— were also occasionally included. The Swedish Gustavian style favored an airy, delicate palette in shades of pearl gray, soft blues, pink, and yellow, bringing light into the northern rooms.

Neoclassical motifs used in painting, plasterwork, wallpaper, and furniture include acanthus and laurel leaves, festoons, guilloches, medallions, urns, rams' heads, tripods, gryphons, curling arabesques, sphinxes, lyres, husks, anthemion (honeysuckle), and palmettes.

EARLY • 19

was coffered or compartmentalized, each coffer or compartment containing a motif or figure created of plasterwork or painted on canvas. Plasterwork was used in a variety of shades: different compartments on ceilings and walls were painted in colors that matched only in tone, while the plasterwork itself was picked out and sometimes gilded.

The fashion for chinoiserie—Western imitations of Chinese art—that first took hold in the late seventeenth century and continued through the eighteenth was another influential resource for the decoration of early neoclassical interiors. The rich, vibrant colors of Chinese lacquer, the inky blues and yellows of porcelain, the delicate pinks and turquoises found on silks and wallpapers from the Orient: all of these colors found their way into neoclassical homes. European adaptations of Chinese decorative patterns—vignettes featuring Chinese people in lush landscape settings, musicians entertaining or young ladies with parasols against a backdrop of pagodas or temple pavilions, or birds and exotic plants, for example—decorated walls and furnishing textiles such as tapestries, bed hangings, coverlets, and upholstery.

COLORS The early neoclassical palette tended to embrace relatively muted colors, often combined with gilding. The colors shown are typical of the period and could be utilized in a great many hues. The muted pale pink could be darkened to a strong rose pink, and the grays and blues were often used together in a variety of tones.

The charming, feminine decorative style of Robert Adam often saw such classical motifs enclosed within round, oval, or rectilinear shapes, a form of decoration used not only for furniture, but also applied to walls, where it found expression in plasterwork or paint. Elaborate patterns and motifs designed by Adam were reinterpreted by skilled craftsmen in delicate plasterwork.

Plasterwork in general tended to be flatter, with less relief than previously, as rhythmic, symmetrical compositions of fragile-looking garlands, arabesques, flowers, and leaves replaced the swirling, asymmetrical scrolls that had gone before. The entire surface of ceilings

LEFT The essence of Gustavian neoclassicism is simplicity. During the final twenty years of the eighteenth century, the style spread beyond royal palaces, and the colors and motifs, laurel swags, festoons, and posies of flowers were found all over Sweden. The subtlety of the decoration is shown by the trompe l'oeil–painted panels and the highlighted pink line. The most copied Gustavian chair has an upholstered seat with rounded corners and turned and fluted legs, and is decorated with carved stylized flowers at the top of the front legs and a floral medallion in the center of the front. Modern reproductions are widely available.

LEFT, BELOW Painted canvas wall panels brought style to spartan rooms at relatively low cost. These wall coverings took over from elaborate and expensive silk. While deriving their inspiration from France, such interiors exhibited a more restrained feel. These trompe l'oeil grisaille panels on a *faux* porphery background depict military, musical, and manual-labor subjects in many tones of gray.

RIGHT The wall decoration here is painted on canvas. In this green salon, the color is typical of the period and compares to Robert Adam's "pea green." The artist delighted in the painting of the room, with every swag and tail slightly different and even highlighted in respect to light coming from the windows. The late-eighteenth-century Gustavian sofa is painted in traditional off-white, with urns and sunflower motifs, and egg-and-dart molding on the friezes.

LEFT Swedish furniture was much influenced by that produced in France. Gustav III studied French culture and language, and traveled on extended visits to France and Italy. This sophistication extended into the Swedish Empire period, when this chest by Jonas Holdstein, fauteuil chairs, candlesticks, and clock were made. The painting of classical ruins by Panini is another pointer to the education and culture of the owner.

BELOW This gilded marble-topped pier table c.1800 has all the motifs and elements of the neoclassical: the urn, sunflowers, and branches with leaves and berries.

FURNITURE

Early neoclassical furniture was typically plain, with straight lines and delicate proportions. It might be painted, or of pale, exotic hardwood—such as satinwood—from the West Indies. These woods were admired for their pale color and dramatic figuring, as were the decorative techniques of marquetry and inlay. In England and America, mahogany was the favored timber for dining chairs and tables.

Highly stylized gilt wooden console tables, with elegant, tapering legs, demi-lune or serpentine tallboys, and upholstered seat furniture of generous proportions feature widely at this time. These were frequently decorated

Although based on a French prototype, this Gustavian sofa has the lightness and purity of its northern roots. Sweden was not as wealthy as France; hence the gilding was replaced by off-white or gray oil-based paint. The upholstery fabric was not silk, but home-woven linen in striped and checked designs: blue, red, or pink, always in conjunction with white. The wide expanse of off-white on the walls, due to the need for as much light as possible in Sweden, produced this quiet, uncomplicated, and elegant style, which remains popular today.

with carved or molded decoration drawn from the classical vocabulary: garlands of flowers, laurel or acanthus leaves, rosettes, medallions, scrolls, or Greek key patterns.

George Hepplewhite's *The Cabinet-Maker and Upholsterer's Guide*, published in 1788, influenced furniture design on both sides of the Atlantic. Bow-fronted chests, chairs with oval and shield backs, and plain vertical fluting are typical of his severely neoclassical designs. These lack the delicate ornamentation of early Adam style, although he does use some Adam motifs, such as urns, festoons, and rosettes. Another book of designs, *The Cabinet Maker and Upholsterer's Drawing Book*, was published by Thomas Sheraton between 1791 and 1794. His rectilinear designs applied Adam motifs as well as French-style lyre shapes and brass galleries on tables and desks, and his book, popular in America, laid the groundwork for Federal style.

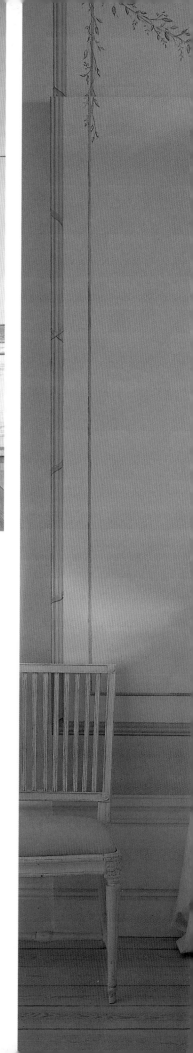

Antique models defined the shapes of decorative objects made of silver, pottery and porcelain, glass, and painted wood. Vase and urn shapes were appropriated for silver tea urns, coffeepots, tureens, and gravy boats, as well as glass tableware and marble clocks. Torchères and candlesticks were often based on ancient incense burners.

In Sweden, the demand for furniture grew as the increasing use of stoves meant that more rooms could be occupied in the cold winter months. Gustavian interiors favored furniture styles popular in France during the reign of Louis XVI, but with less gilding, and often painted in shades of pale yellow or gray. A typical Gustavian chair boasted an upholstered seat with rounded corners, turned legs, and carved, stylized flowers. Sofas were ample, with simply turned or tapered legs and carved or molded classical ornament—garlands, egg-and-dart or Greek key motifs, and laurel leaves.

ABOVE The twenty-first-century love of white, off-white, cream, and some shades of gray, with just a hint of classical refinement, has meant that Scandinavian style, and particularly Gustavian design, is very much in demand. This sofa is an exact replica of a Gustavian piece, with the colors in tune with modern taste. The faience is modern and is made in France.

RIGHT A corner of a dining room furnished completely with modern Gustavian and Directoire pieces. These are styles that sit well together: the influence for both came from France, but in Sweden they were simplified and given this particular Swedish light and airy feel. The chairs are dressed with thin white cotton, and all glassware, ceramics, and flatware are modern copies.

OPPOSITE Gustavian style sits very happily in an early Connecticut house. The Swedish style, with a more rustic look than its French counterpart, suits the bare, wide floorboards and solid beams.

ROOMS

The elegance of the Roman style was echoed in the sleek, graceful lines of eighteenth-century interiors. Italy remains at the heart of Robert Adam's neoclassicism: his interiors were light, bright, and delicate, and the design of the floor, ceiling, walls, and furniture was all closely related. Colorful carpet designs were linked harmoniously with painted and stuccoed ceilings. Pier tables stood below pier glass, flanked by urns. Rooms and the furniture in them were comprised of geometric shapes—squares, rectangles, ovals, and circles—unified by the decorative scheme, with great attention paid to the tiniest detail.

Gustavian interiors tend to be well proportioned, but spare in relation to their furnishings, with the plentiful woods of Scandinavia used to underscore a quiet, uncomplicated, ordered, and elegant effect. Floors might be covered with planks of scrubbed pine or inlaid patterns of parquet, or painted to resemble stone blocking. The characteristic frosty Scandinavian palette—comprised of pinks, yellow, greens, soft blue, and off-white—is used on paneled walls that are then decorated with classical motifs or given a rustic touch by using paint effects to imitate porphyry. Tiled stoves, sometimes in the shape of classical columns, were characteristic. Besides mural paintings, favored materials for wall decoration included canvas painted with trompe l'oeil classical motifs, printed calico, and woven linens in striped or checked designs. In an effort to use the available light to best advantage, tall windows were dressed with delicate, thin cotton curtains in white or pale color schemes.

Graceful elliptical rooms and circular flying staircases—perhaps with balusters and newel posts shaped as columns, vases, or human figures, or embellished with classical ornament such as wreaths or scrollwork—reflecting the curvilinear quality of the decorative features characterize interiors designed in the Federal style in America. Walls were generally painted in the pale palette of white, pink, and lavender, but with the addition of more vivid shades of bright blues, greens, and yellows.

In the late eighteenth century, growing numbers of European and American travelers to Greece and southern Italy observed ancient architecture firsthand. A Greek revival followed, emphasizing purity of form. Where Adam style had taken Greek vocabulary of ornament and combined it eclectically with Roman shapes and motifs, now a more authentic interpretation of antiquities was favored.

GRAND NEOCLASSICAL

When Louis XVI ascended the French throne in 1774, neoclassical fashion was favoring lighter forms and leaning toward the ornament of Greek temples: palmettes, anthemia, and bucrania. But as Greece became more accessible to the Grand Tourist, books on antiquity furnished an introduction to authentic neoclassical architecture and ornament, with widely circulated pattern books also providing ideas. Thomas Sheraton's *Cabinet Dictionary* of 1803 included large scrolls and volutes, claw and paw feet, and lion masks—features of the developing Regency style—along with continuing elements of Louis XVI neoclassicism such as *colonnettes*, fluting, and ribbon borders.

In the 1790s, after the French Revolution, the luxurious French Empire style—classical, exotic, and faithful to the precedents of ancient Greece and Egypt—was created for Napoleon Bonaparte by the architects and designers Charles Percier and Pierre-François Fontaine.

English Regency style, popular in Britain from the late 1790s until the late 1830s, depended heavily on French Empire style, turning away from lighter Adam and Hepplewhite designs. In both Britain and France, the new neoclassical fashion emphasized authentic classical forms rather than merely taking the decorative ornament of the classical past. But where French Empire style drew on Rome, English Regency combined Roman motifs with classical Greek and Etruscan elements.

In America, enthusiasm for French Empire style flourished, reaching fashionable heights in the 1820s and 1830s. Austria and Germany adopted a less pompous, more functional version of French Empire known as Biedermeier, popular from the late 1820s, while in Sweden the taste for French architecture and decoration championed by Gustav III continued in the early years of the nineteenth century with Swedish Empire style.

OPPOSITE: TOP LEFT This section of a plaster model for the portal of a basilica in Rome has potent classical symbols: the shell, a winged putto, volutes, and a garland of husks or bellflowers.

TOP RIGHT The scrolled arm supports on this Louis XVI fauteuil chair have acanthus molding terminating with rosettes, and the frame has garlands of husks and egg-and-dart carving. These simple decorative devices place this chair firmly in the neoclassical revival of the mid-eighteenth century.

BOTTOM LEFT An early-eighteenth-century gilt-bronze mount on a French Regency black lacquer table. The iconography of classicism is again displayed: a rosette with scrolling leaf forms and a female head with a wreath of oak leaves, which is essentially late Baroque/classical revival.

BOTTOM RIGHT A pair of early-eighteenth-century French Regency gilded bronze candlesticks, chased with swirling acanthus scrolls. This exudes the Rococo style favored during this period.

LEFT The centerpiece to this room is the eighteenth-century marble fireplace with lamps and urns. The classical theme is further accentuated by the Greek key border and molding on the apple-green velvet walls. This pattern is mirrored in the carpet. The unusual chairs are Regency Anglo-Afghan campaign chairs with "dancing" feet. The rare early-nineteenth-century prints are of Napoleonic battle formations.

BELOW The interior of this house in London designed by Frédéric Méchiche was originally built between 1728 and 1759, and was reworked in 1845. The *piano nobile*, the upper floor used for entertaining, has simple paneling painted in muted colors and a spectacular marble fireplace with a dentil edge, swag-and-tail decoration, and Greek key pattern.

ARCHITECTURE

The neoclassicism of both French Empire style, fashionable throughout Europe, and English Regency emphasized strict adherence to classical forms. The main influences were ancient Greece and Egypt, although the architectural ornament of Imperial Rome was also adopted in celebration of Napoleon's military might. Both styles relied on ancient motifs, including palm trees, sphinxes, lions, Greek caryatids, and the Imperial eagle. Interiors featured columns, pilasters, and architraves.

Alongside French Empire and English Regency, another strand of neoclassicism— Greek Revival—made an impact on European architecture and interior design from the 1780s, inspired by ancient Greek buildings excavated

in the late eighteenth century. Purity and austerity of form define Greek Revival interiors. Grander Greek Revival houses often boasted both domed ceilings and coffered flat ceilings. Fashionable designs for ceiling medallions and borders included combinations of Greek motifs such as guilloches and rosettes, while plain wall panels were occasionally embellished with medallions inspired by Greek originals.

During the early nineteenth century, French neoclassical taste exerted considerable influence across the Atlantic. But while French Empire style drew on classical Rome, the exteriors of many new houses in America began to reflect the fashion for classical Greek architecture. The late 1830s saw Greek Revival style adopted for interiors as well, as it had been through much of Europe. By this time American neoclassical architecture and decoration had developed an identity separate from its European sources of inspiration, with the integration of native motifs —corn cobs, tobacco leaves, stars, and the bald eagle—giving it a distinctive American flavor.

ABOVE Michael Coorengel and Jean Pierre Calvagrac have chosen a series of colors to accentuate the architectural details of their Parisian apartment. The paneling is painted a matt blue, while the acanthus detailing in the molding is picked out in white.

LEFT This style can be quite simply achieved in a bedroom with good color choice, the application of two pilasters— either antique or reproductions—a suite of chairs in keeping with the period, and a headboard made from a large gilt picture frame.

COLOR AND PATTERN

Houses decorated in the grander, more opulent version of neoclassical style have traditionally relied upon bold colors and confident patterns to make a statement, even if that statement was born in the twenty-first century rather than being a faithful document of what came before. What matters above all else is the rendering of a tradition that celebrates the courageous spirit of antiquity. It does not matter if the warm, rich colors that evoke the hospitable elegance of a noble Roman *domus* are chosen, or the subtle, cool palette found in a grand farmhouse in Sweden, so long as the color creates a mood and blends with classically inspired taste.

The color palette of the French Empire and English Regency periods tended to be vivid, somewhat daring, and extensive. A color that often assumed pride of place was crimson,

frequently embellished or enlivened with gilded detailing, and celebrating the desire to create richly appointed, jewellike interiors. Along with being universally recommended for dining rooms, red was also considered the most appropriate backdrop for fine paintings, and was used in libraries as well. Libraries and drawing rooms happily accommodated the color green, while various shades of blue found a home in the bedroom. Frequently colors were selected according to the position of the rooms. Shades of blue and green were thought to be appropriate for south-facing chambers, while those with a northern exposure were given warmth with a palette of buff, pink, or red—especially in north-facing bedrooms, where floral wallpapers enjoyed favor.

As time passed, lighter hues became fashionable. Pinks, blues, buff, lilacs, and French grays were frequently combined with contrasting colors in more vibrant versions. Marbling and

ABOVE The Parisian interior designer Frédéric Méchiche is well known for his use of dramatic black-and-white stripes on wallpaper and fabric. Some have said that the popularity of the strong stripe was due to the stripes on Napoleon's campaign tents, but the device is equally powerful in deep red, green, blue, or yellow. Here the fabric is applied to a late-eighteenth-century painted and gilt window seat.

LEFT This blue on the paneling has a more modern feel than the traditional deep, bright blue associated with high Regency. The scene is set by the wonderful French Empire chaise longue with the crimson-red and gold fabric. This room perfectly blends the traditional color palette with a more modern appeal.

RIGHT The classical need not be in opposition to the modern. Here a modern classic—a painting by Damien Hirst—adds a new dimension to the icons of classicism: the Adam-style candlestick and the 18th-century marble fireplace with rosette, Ionic capital, and Greek key-pattern frieze.

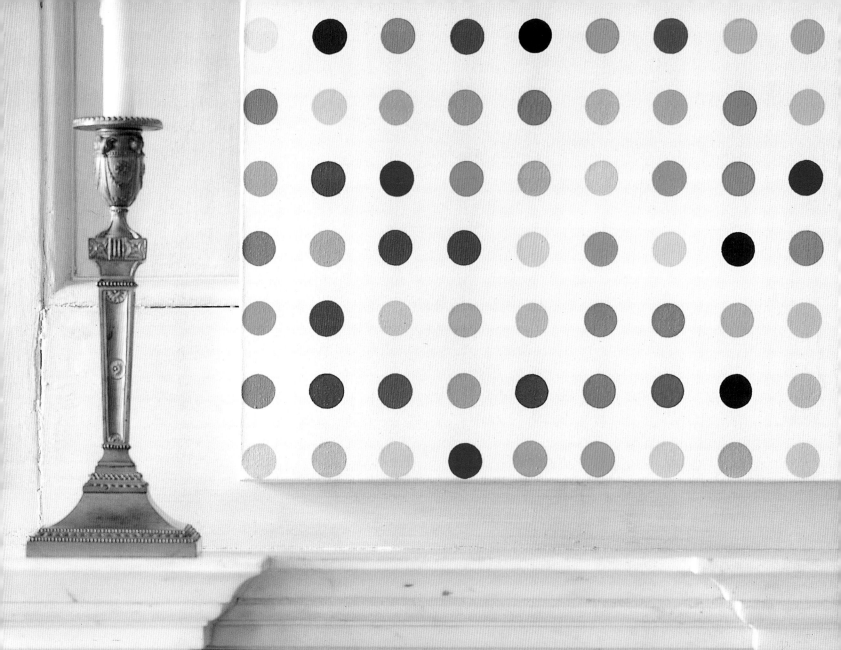

LEFT The secret of neoclassicism is the use of opulent color and pattern, as shown here in an interior by Juan Pablo Molyneux. The richness of the apple-green velvet on the walls and the Greek key pattern on the walls and carpet immediately give visual clues to the desired style. This is emphasized by the small console table with ormolu mounts, made in the workshops of Bernard Molitor (c.1730–1833), one of the great *ébénistes* who created such furniture for Napoleon I. Prints, such as these of Napoleon's war formations, add to the strong classical statement, as do the bronze urns.

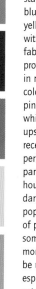

COLORS As grand neoclassicism is exuberant and full of self-confidence, colors should reflect this. The late-eighteenth- and early-nineteenth-century colorists loved strong statements. Crimson, strong blue, bright green, and yellow, often combined with gold or used in striped fabrics and wall coverings, proved popular, particularly in receiving rooms. Lighter colors such as paler blues, pinks, buffs, and off-whites were often used upstairs, spreading to reception rooms as the period progressed, particularly in grand rural houses. (In urban areas, dark colors remained popular due to the effects of pollution.) As seen in some of our locations, more modern colors can be used successfully, especially with highly saturated colors.

ABOVE Off-whites, grays, and various shades of pale blue, with picked-out gilding, have been used in neoclassical interiors, following the French taste, since the eighteenth century. Combined with simple paneling, painted and gilt furniture, which has been popular in France from the same period, and with silks or even animal-print fabrics, a unified scheme can be created in a modern setting.

ABOVE RIGHT Pattern is often ignored in creating interior styles, but was extremely important to the classicists. This complex velvet wall covering by Sabina Fay Braxton is a series of hand-dyed panels emulating marble, along with patterns consistent with the theme.

graining were popular wall treatments, as were wallpapers in florals and stripes and—for very grand houses—Chinese wallpapers. Rich, fine-quality wallpapers were particularly used in drawing rooms, dining rooms, and libraries. As an integral part of the overall decorative scheme, floor coverings were also important, with Turkish-patterned carpets or geometric patterns loosely based on Roman mosaic pavements among the most popular choices.

The practice of matching curtains to upholstery, with floor coverings and walls in harmonizing colors, remained fashionable during the first quarter of the nineteenth century. In general, light colors such as lilac and lemon yellow were favored, and nearly always a combination of two colors prevailed for curtains. Among the most popular combinations were blue and lilac, French gray with amber,

and light green and pink. Elaborate fringes, tassels, and cords in gold or yellow complemented the gilding of the furniture and picture frames.

Patterns for everything from wallpaper and paneling ornament to the moldings of fireplace surrounds drew inspiration from the majestic architectural elements of classical antiquity. Bold stripes, Greek key patterns, and mosaiclike geometric designs all contrasted in color with encrusted decoration such as seashells, garlands, and *paterae* (oval dish shapes). Among such patterns still popular today, for walls and furniture ornament alike, are the Greek meander, the anthemion or acanthus leaf, and Ionic columns. These references to antiquity create an ambience of solidity and tradition, an effective backdrop for experimental modern themes.

FURNITURE

The archaeological excavations in Greece and southern Italy, along with Napoleon's military campaigns in Egypt, proved pivotal in the development of new styles of furniture in the early nineteenth century. No longer content simply to combine a variety of decorative elements drawn from the classical vocabulary, designers rose to the challenge of creating original furniture whose shape depended heavily on archaeological authenticity. Looking to the classical past, many pieces were styled after shapes discovered in the ruins of houses excavated at Pompeii and Herculaneum, for example, or depicted on ancient Greek vases.

The Greek Revival introduced an item of furniture that became not only central to the Empire style in France, but also popular in Regency England and America: the Greek *klismos* chair. With outcurving saber legs and a concave back, its robust shape was well suited to a comfortable, well-appointed interior. In England a version of this elegant design was

RIGHT The front elevation of an architectural sofa (with a totally flat back and curved front) made for the Comte d'Artois by the Parisian cabinetmaker Georges Jacob (1739–1814), who was particularly known for his craftsmanship and carving. On this sofa, the classical motifs are the lion's head with mane, and foot with deeply carved claws.

CLOCKWISE FROM TOP LEFT The X-frame stool was first made in ancient Egypt. It was common in Europe during the Renaissance, and was revived in Europe and North America in the neoclassical revival of the early nineteenth century. It would originally have been gilded; the fashion for animal-print fabrics is contemporary.

On this crisply carved torchère, remnants of original gilding adorn the guilloche molding, with swags of husks and berries.

This gilded, nineteenth-century French chair, with simple bead molding and rosettes, has been upholstered in a fabric complementary to the iridescent taffeta drapes.

French furniture of the eighteenth century exudes restrained classical reference, from the small black lacquer French Regency table with ormolu mounts to the gilded French Empire fauteuils. Although furniture of this quality is quite rare, it is possible to create a similar effect with furniture produced in the late nineteenth and early twentieth centuries.

adapted for the "Trafalgar" parlor chair, decorated with rope-turning and Egyptian motifs in honor of Lord Nelson's victory at the Battle of the Nile. Another shape that also found favor for chairs and stools took its form from the Roman curule, with X-form, double-curved legs. Like chairs, sofas tended to be adaptations of ancient Greek models depicted on Greek vases. Generously proportioned, with graceful, elegant lines, a sofa might have scrolling ends and curved legs, or boldly carved lion-paw feet. Other popular variations included the comfortable chaise longue, a style featuring a low end with a short scrolled arm.

French Empire chairs, stools, and sofas were often richly embellished with motifs that

ABOVE AND LEFT The apple-green velvet on the walls, the large modern painting by De Juan, the prints of Piranesi's column, and the furs, skins, and silks serve as a backdrop to the collection of classically inspired, and in particular Egyptian-inspired, furniture. The French Empire *bergère* has winged-sphinx arm supports. The ancient Greek sphinx had a woman's head and breasts, a lion's body, often wings, and was thought of as a source of enigmatic wisdom. Highly appropriate for a library chair!

celebrated the military achievements of Napoleon: swags and trophies, the eagle of Imperial Rome, Egyptian gods and sphinxes, and caryatids and lotus leaves inspired by the Nile campaigns. A common motif was the mask of the god Apollo which, as the emblem of the Sun King, served as a powerful reminder of Napoleon's place in history.

During the English Regency and French Empire periods, a variety of new table forms in classical or Egyptian style were introduced. Among the most popular were circular library or dining tables and gaming or console tables, all resting on supports that looked to antiquity for inspiration. A single pedestal, winged lion or griffin monopodia, classical lyres, full caryatids or terms headed by Egyptian masks now found favor. Robust trestles resembling the ends of Roman sarcophagi supported writing tables. Other table styles that were introduced at this time included drum tables, sofa tables, and the Carlton House desk.

While mahogany remained a popular wood, glossy rosewood imported from South America and the Caribbean was widely used for English

Regency and French Empire furniture. Other woods commonly used for veneers included maple and boldly figured, prized zebra wood or amboyna. Among the more popular decorative touches for furniture were the application of gilding, ormolu mounts, and inlay of brass or exotic woods such as ebony.

Sumptuous fabrics and trimmings, which played an important role in the decoration of interiors on both sides of the Atlantic in the early nineteenth century, were especially instrumental in the design of beds. Among the more popular styles was one that drew inspiration from the tent or field beds of military campaigns, with draperies forming a tent or canopy around a framework; this was

ABOVE (AND ABOVE LEFT) This bed, with its sensational pharaoh's-head pilasters with stylized claw feet, may look French Empire in date, but it is in fact late eighteenth century and was probably made in England. The influence on top cabinetmakers of Egyptian style was at its greatest in the second half of the eighteenth century.

LEFT A Directoire flame mahogany library chair with lion's-head arm supports sweeping down to finely carved claw feet.

FAR LEFT Many firms today produce excellent reproductions of antique furniture. This nineteenth-century-style French trundle bed was made in Paris to order and exported to New York. The drapes around the bed are new Fortuny fabric, and the cushions are made from old Fortuny fabric. The overall effect is of late-nineteenth-century French neoclassicism.

LEFT Much of the classical feel in this bedroom comes from the yellow-and-cream, striped silk wall covering. The early-eighteenth-century bombé marquetry chest, eighteenth-century bronze urns on marble bases, and Dutch oil painting, dated 1570, give a scholarly feel.

particularly suitable for small rooms in fashionable villas and cottages. Another trendsetting bed was in the very elegant French style: essentially a sofa, it was placed sideways against a wall, with lavish folds of drapes falling from a small canopy attached to the ceiling.

A combination of English and French influence, the American Empire style was brought to a wide audience by the furniture maker Duncan Phyfe. In German-speaking countries, the Biedermeier style avoided the ostentation of French Empire and English Regency fashions, with furniture boasting broad expanses of veneers made of pale local fruitwoods such as walnut, cherry, and birch, sparely decorated with simple bands of inlay.

Since the early nineteenth century, the bold designs of French Empire and English Regency furniture have continuously found favor for interiors throughout Europe and the United States. Solid, confident, and assertive, this grand neoclassical fashion nonetheless marries well with more delicate or exotic forms.

OPPOSITE, ABOVE Frédéric Méchiche has taken a classic early-19th-century daybed and covered it in a very suitable striped fabric. What gives this an airy modern feel is his choice of color—parma violet. This is also reflected in the wall color.

RIGHT The walls in this salon in New York, designed by Juan Pablo Molyneux, have been painted a very, very pale lavender, almost ice but with warmth. It serves as a backdrop to the series of twelve seventeenth-century French bronze Roman emperors. The eighteenth-century gilt-wood sofa by Georges Jacob is covered in complementary striped silk fabric. The Aubusson carpet provides a more feminine feel.

ARTIFACTS

Classical antiquity provided a wealth of source material for decorative artifacts. Objects such as the lyre of Apollo, the obelisk, and the tripod captured the popular imagination and inspired many decorative artifacts, including gilt-bronze clocks and lamps. The grandeur of antiquity also manifested itself in designs for porcelain and silver objects, including vases, teaware, and tableware. Silver and porcelain tableware in particular relied heavily on classical forms.

French Empire silver is dominated by bold profiles, embellished with a disciplined application of ornament and enhanced by cast sculptural elements. By the early nineteenth century, Egyptian motifs were fashionable, reflecting the military exploits of Napoleon. Regency silver in England, championed by the workshops of Paul Storr and Rundell, Bridge and Rundell, also adopted antique prototypes, albeit heavier and more sculptural versions.

In ceramics, Empire vases were broader versions of original Egyptian and Etruscan shapes. The ceramics produced in England by Josiah Wedgwood emulated decorative motifs found on ancient Greek vases, including lions, sphinxes, birds, mythical harpies, and griffins.

The density of ornament during the Empire and Regency periods was in marked contrast to Biedermeier style, where French Empire shapes were stripped of their elaborate decoration. Biedermeier ceramics, silver, and glass comprised simplified classical shapes, typically embellished with thick gilding and painted with sentimental scenes in colorful enamels.

In Greek Revival style, pride of place went to busts and sculptures of gods and goddesses fashioned in bronze or marble, along with vases and urns. Some were original, but most were reproductions of classical Greek and Etruscan wares unearthed in archaeological excavations.

ABOVE Cups and saucers made in hard-paste porcelain at the Marieburg porcelain factory outside Stockholm in the 1780s.

RIGHT The symmetry of obelisks, with work of art above, is given added interest by a grouping of early green glass.

RIGHT, BELOW A harlequin collection of fine white porcelain and glass decorated with gilding gives an opulent theme to this dining table of Coorengel and Calvagrac.

THIS PAGE To glory in and wonder at the human body has been a recurrent theme in the art of the classics. A vast number of bronzes have been produced throughout the centuries, with the zenith being the late nineteenth and early twentieth centuries.

ABOVE The clever positioning of this small bronze in a gilt-wood frame belies its importance. It is a late-sixteenth-century Venetian bronze of Apollo from the school of Alessandro Vittoria, and once belonged to the Emperor Franz Josef of Austria.

RIGHT This finely carved wooden head of Caesar by Professor Poeltzl from Dresden, c.1920, again glories in the beauty of the ancient Romans.

LEFT Two bronzes of "The Ball Balancer" by Max Levi, c.1920, rejoice in the fine physique of the athletes of ancient Rome, in front of an oil painting, "The Death of Tristan," by Stolz.

RIGHT This bronze is titled "The Archer" by E. M. Geyger, c.1890. The artist made an larger-than-life-size model for Kaiser Wilhelm II, which now stands in Potsdam.

ROOMS

Life during the period of the English Regency was considerably less formal than that enjoyed by generations past, and the architecture and arrangement of interiors reflected this. Rooms tended to be small, with low ceilings, and frequently boasted an attractive bay window. Rather than being arranged around the room, furniture was assembled near the fireplace. Light filled rooms like never before, with the new, efficient oil lamps enabling several people to share a table for reading or writing.

On the whole, Regency rooms were light and graceful, given to fairly plain walls painted in a clear, pale color and occasionally featuring a narrow border. Ceilings were usually left plain, or perhaps decorated with a small central garland, from which a chandelier was suspended.

Among the many celebrated innovations of the French Empire designers Charles Percier and Pierre-François Fontaine was the lavish use of fabric draperies for interior decoration. Typical of French Empire style was the coordination of soft

furnishings in both fabric and color, with the carpet of a room echoing the decoration on the walls. Beds, and even entire rooms, were swathed with rich, sumptuous fabrics, re-creating the tented dwellings of military campaigns. Opulent rooms were fashioned by looping silks and velvets in voluptuous sweeps over valances and on the framework of beds. Small rooms imitated tents, with fabrics draped across the walls and suspended from the ceiling. When fabric was not used to flank rooms, the fashion for patterned wallpapers took over from wall paintings.

In keeping with this penchant for lavish drapery, the design of curtains began to play a key role in decorative schemes for the interior. Often a pole was extended across the entire width of the tall, floor-level windows, and material was draped around it, in graceful folds or very elaborate pointed drops. The floor-length drapes and curtains were frequently lined in a contrasting color that would be artfully displayed by the draping.

ABOVE Michael Coorengel and Jean Pierre Calvagrac have used a dramatic gray-black with gilding to set off their collection of French Empire antiques. The stark white pedestal and urn reflect the ceiling and floor covering, and seem to make a statement of the classical inspiration.

LEFT In his apartment in Munich, Heinrich Graf von Spreti has skillfully combined the classical with the Oriental, in artifacts and colors. The room is dominated by the mid-eighteenth-century Parisian mirrors and classical bronze figures, clocks, lights, and paintings. But the cabinets and contrasting red and black fabrics are straight from the Orient. As an added individual touch, the leopard-print daybed came from a hotel in Casablanca.

An appealing addition to the neoclassical interior was the conservatory, which most frequently opened out of the drawing room or library. The desire to bring the outside into the home, which had originated in England with the garden designer Humphrey Repton, also saw rooms decorated with panoramic landscape views or architectural settings, or painted to resemble the inside of an aviary.

An interior decorated in grand neoclassical style can be at once lavish and bold. Plain wall paneling painted in light colors and bordered with a simple dentil or ovolo molding provides the perfect foil for bright, spirited paintings. A spacious setting gives voice to sofas and chairs upholstered with luscious, sensuous fabrics in exotic patterns and writing tables, cabinets, and desks veneered with precious materials—such as lacquer—or embellished with gilding.

But the decoration of rooms need not be locked in the past, paying obsequious homage to the majesty of classical antiquity. The strength of this style lies in the details—a marble floor patterned with a time-honored ancient motif, a mirror bordered with fluted pilasters, the Corinthian columns of a fireplace surround, or moldings ornamented with the Greek key pattern. A neoclassical interior furnishes a fitting backdrop against which to combine a variety of styles and add what is unique or unusual—perhaps modern paintings and sculpture, tribal artifacts, or a Chinese apothecary's cabinet. This is a style that comfortably celebrates the virtues of what has gone before at the same time as joyfully embracing what is new, a quality that renders it an ideal and eternally modern choice for a twenty-first-century interior.

LEFT In this bathroom in London by Frédéric Méchiche, classic simplicity reigns: notice the wide black and white stripes, the key-pattern molding, and the marble floor star, which was inspired by the Romans.

RIGHT In Méchiche's bathroom in Paris, period authenticity permeates the eighteenth-century Directoire style, with the *faux*-wooden zinc-lined bathtub and the two Directoire grisaille landscape panels flanked by pilasters. The walls are *faux* marble. But there are also touches of modernity: the classic Bertoia chairs and modern painting.

The taste for simpler neoclassical style came to the fore in the eighteenth and, primarily, the nineteenth centuries. Its essence was restraint, incorporating elements from other faces of neoclassicism, but applying them in a quietly purist manner. This style heralds classical forms born in the antique past: the plain, clean lines inherent in the architecture and furnishings of antiquity inform the tranquil, well-proportioned interior.

SIMPLE NEOCLASSICAL

Throughout the eighteenth century there had been strong leanings toward classicism of one sort or another, and neoclassical taste had been encouraged by the archaeological discoveries in southern Italy, at Pompeii and Herculaneum, and again as doors opened up for travelers to Greece. The clean, classic lines that define this simple form of neoclassical style look back to what fundamentally adheres to the tenets first set down in the writings of the ancient Roman architect Vitruvius.

Set in the context of this pared-down, uncluttered approach, the ingredients that were mixed together to make up the style— whose inherent simplicity makes a strong, straightforward statement—echoed a variety of historical traditions. Certain decorative elements of an interior might rely heavily upon architectural forms found in the buildings and furnishings of ancient Greece and Rome: a lamp base patterned after an Ionic column, for

example, or a table leg in the shape of a dignified, sculptural lion. At the same time, its ornamental features might also look to other stylistic traditions derived from antiquity, such as the Italian Renaissance, as well as the French Empire and English Regency periods that predominated in grander neoclassical interiors. Imaginative combinations of objects —an architectural fragment from a column base sharing space with a piece of contemporary sculpture, for instance—helped to create an atmosphere that was at once as comfortable with the accessories of the past as with the accoutrements of more modern life.

It is hardly surprising that the simple neoclassical interior seduces, challenging traditional ideas of decorating by proffering impressive and imaginative alternatives to what is traditionally thought of as classical while celebrating the understated, the elegant, and the harmonious.

OPPOSITE: TOP LEFT The legs of this table are made from cast bronze in the traditional form of a lion's head with mane and a claw foot.

TOP RIGHT This tablescape is proof that the classical can sit happily with other styles. The walnut 18th-century table is English, the marble head is of the Roman statesman Cato, the small trinket box is French, and the neon lamp is 1960s Italian. Even in this combination, the effect is of restrained classicism.

BOTTOM LEFT This early paneling and fire-surround from an early-eighteenth-century Georgian townhouse in London is totally understated. It is given an uncharacteristic Scandinavian feel with gray and white paint.

BOTTOM RIGHT The eagle as an icon dates from Assyrian times, when it denoted power and victory. It has been used as a symbol by Roman legions, the Holy Roman Empire, the Austro-Hungarian Empire, the United States, France under Napoleon, Prussia, Poland, and Nazi Germany—an instantly recognizable classical symbol.

COLOR AND PATTERN

On the whole, simpler neoclassical interiors tend to favor paler or more muted colors than their grander counterparts. This preference for neutral hues highlights the feeling of serenity and clarity of a space, while calling attention to other decorative elements such as textures, scale, and the form of furniture and objects. A palette of light grays and shades of cream and off-white for walls, floors, and ceilings does not reduce the interior to bland monotony, but provides a fitting backdrop that allows the imaginative placement of furnishings and decorative objects to take pride of place.

Confident use of geometric, architectural shapes for furniture or wall decoration adds drama and flair to a quietly simple room.

Against a neutral background, the bright colors and patterns of a painting, the rich dark patina of a wooden cabinet, or the bold vivid designs of a carpet stand out in dramatic display. Materials that look back to classical antiquity and are adopted for furnishings also add a colorful dimension and depth to the decorative scheme of the simple neoclassical interior; such quotations from the antique include the warm, gleaming patina of bronze, the cool, variegated surface of polished marble and limestone, and the luminous radiance of gilding.

The architecture of a room can also be called upon as a decorative device. The plain, geometrical shapes of windows, doors, wainscoting, and fire surrounds create patterns that echo the spirit of classical simplicity. To the discerning eye, even the arrangement of pictures on a wall, an architectural mirror, or the manner in which objects are placed on a table or cupboard might conjure a provocative design that brings a graphic character to an interior, evoking the harmony and purity endemic in ancient Greece and Rome.

LEFT In a house in New York State built in the 1870s, a straw yellow has been used in the main receiving room. This color works well with the gilding on the frame and the girandole candleholder; a slight color-wash gives a softer look.

LEFT, BELOW In the same house in the dining room, a dramatic coral color-wash effect suits the white-painted furniture and textiles. Reds have always been regarded as dining colors. The original pressed-tin ceiling has been painted white.

FAR RIGHT Pale to mid blues have long been associated with classical interiors, particularly when combined with creams and buffs. In this hallway a trompe l'oeil raised and fielded paneled dado is created by use of light and dark shades.

COLORS A simple style with neoclassical overtones can fit well with a backdrop of white, off-white, grays, creams, and pale tones of yellow and blue. All of these allow the furniture and decorative features to make the statement. However, deeper colors, such as warm orange-red, can also work when twinned with simple and classically elegant furniture.

The color palette of this late-nineteenth-century house in New York State is made up of grays and neutrals. Eliminating color change does not reduce a house to sameness, but allows other elements such as texture, scale, and form to come into play. The star motif became particularly popular during the Regency and Federal periods.

LEFT This room is dominated by the early-nineteenth-century daybed with inlaid acanthus leaves and lozenges. The open armchair is late Regency, c.1830. The neutral colors and painted wooden floor serve as a backdrop to the classical prints and simple architectural details.

RIGHT The furnishings in this room have been mainly flea-market finds. It is the juxtaposition of the painted plaster bust, the nineteenth-century French campaign bed, the simple nineteenth-century armoire painted with black over red and then waxed, the plain gray-painted table—all set against the white-painted background, reminiscent of white marble—that gives it a calming, classical feel.

BELOW This 1940s French chair with plain cream upholstery allows the eye to light on the mid-nineteenth-century French prints by Deley of the "Restoration of the Temple of the Sun in Rome."

FURNITURE

The furniture that decorated the simple neoclassical interior paid homage to the classical styles of the historical past while creating a fresh, comfortable space for living. It embraced many forms of classicism, drawing inspiration from ancient Greece and Rome, the Italian Renaissance, and the English Regency and French Empire periods. No single style was considered to be more authentic than another, but rather each was looked to for common threads of purity and simplicity, for strong lines using a minimum of decorative ornament.

One of the most effective means of dressing a simple neoclassical interior was by using furniture that evoked the classical past but did not derive solely from it. This was accomplished

with a variety of methods, such as taking elements from the dictionary of antique design and the vocabulary of antique ornament and adapting and applying them in striking and original ways. Examples of such an approach might include a round table top made of *faux* granite supported by a classical urn; a daybed with the clean, pure lines of a Roman banqueting couch and embellished with carvings of antique motifs such as laurel and acanthus leaves, scrolling foliage, or a lozenge pattern; or a plain, utterly simple chair that drew inspiration from an English Regency design (which itself looked back to the Roman curule chair but remains thoroughly contemporary)—these are the kinds of classical quotations that were well suited to an interior that was decorated along the clean and simple lines that inform neoclassical taste.

Many pieces of classically inspired furniture that were especially at home in a simple interior looked to the late-eighteenth-century designs of Robert Adam, Thomas Sheraton, and George

RIGHT Within an overall classical interior, a nineteenth-century gilt-wood French open-arm chair alludes to an earlier Rococo style.

FAR RIGHT Frank Faulkner is someone who rejoices in honest damage. He finds the fact that this early-nineteenth-century chair shows the effects of a hard life merely adds to its beauty and interest.

LEFT There are many ways of interpreting a classical style. This wonderful cabinet has all the elements of Biedermeier style, fashionable in Germany, Austria, and Scandinavia from c.1815 to c.1850. It was, however, designed by Charles Eastlake much later in the nineteenth century.

RIGHT Although often made in light-colored maple, Biedermeier chests were also constructed in flame mahogany. A classical cameo can be created by the careful placement of prints, plaster medallions, a bronze urn-shaped lamp, and an iconic ram's head.

BELOW Simplicity in color and form can establish a style. Here a Victorian mahogany bombé-fronted chest, with plaster bust, Victorian dressing mirror, and Syrian box give the feeling of a traveler's collection. The marble urn sets the scene.

Hepplewhite. A gilded chair with slender fluted legs or vase-shaped splats, and the delicate, gracefully proportioned demi-lune side table are engaging examples of sophistication and elegance well suited to a simply furnished room.

The furniture of the English Regency and French Empire periods, such as chairs based upon the Greek *klismos*, with outcurved saber legs and a concave back, or chairs and stools patterned after the Roman curule with X-form, double-curved legs and single-pedestal tables, are among the designs that were seen to best advantage in the simple neoclassical interior if left plain and undecorated. Yet the heavy, florid ornament that drew inspiration from the motifs celebrating the military victories of Napoleon—

ABOVE Frank Faulkner's painting, a simple pine table with bronze lamps, a nautilus shell, and two nineteenth-century X-frame stools are all part of the logic and clarity Frank believes is the essence of the classical.

RIGHT The large bronze lion's-head and claw-foot legs of this table are nineteenth century. The leather top was designed by the owner, Andrea Truglio. The deliberate starkness of the interior, with strong lines and no decoration, serves to accentuate the strong lines of the furniture.

sphinxes, caryatids, and trophies, for example—could also be successfully integrated into the decorative scheme of a simple neoclassical room. A chair with armrests in the form of the Imperial eagle might be painted white, or a tabletop covered in pale-colored leather could be supported by four dignified lion monopodia.

Simple neoclassical is also at home with the Biedermeier style of furniture that was fashionable in Germany and Austria in the early nineteenth century. Veneered with sweeping fields of fruitwoods and sparsely decorated with a minimum of ornament, cupboards, chests, and armoires married effortlessly with other classical forms, and found ready accommodation in a light, pale-colored room.

LEFT Classicism is frequently associated with collecting. The Grand Tours of the eighteenth and nineteenth centuries meant that many different elements found their way into homes in Europe and America.

BELOW A plaster head, from the studio of Antonio Canova (1757–1822), is protected from further damage by a modern vase.

ARTIFACTS

Decorative objects were expressive vehicles for pared-down neoclassical style. In general these ornaments took their inspiration from the artifacts of classical antiquity—bronze vessels and urns, red-and-black painted pottery vases, architectural columns, or furnishings such as tripods or curule chairs—but refused to imitate them slavishly. A marble Corinthian column, for example, might be chosen as an appropriate base for a lamp. The bust of a Roman emperor, engravings of archaeological ruins reminiscent of the work of Piranesi, a large bronze urn, or stucco wall ornaments patterned after the

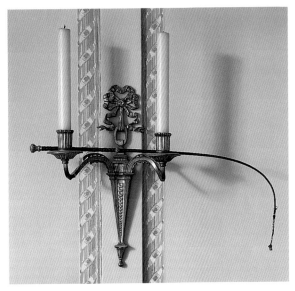

roundels of Greek coins and medals—these are decorative objects that suggest an admiration for the antique, but do not copy directly from it.

Alongside these quotations from classical antiquity were objects that invoked the spirit of Italian Renaissance references to classicism, such as bronze wall plaques or terracotta sculptures of Olympian gods—another strong but very different connection with ancient Greece and Rome. Still others were lifted from the bold and majestic thread of neoclassicism favored during the French Empire and English Regency periods: ceramics and silver tableware in strong, sculptural shapes based on antique

forms, for example, or Egyptian motifs such as the obelisk or sphinx gave a dramatic and confident twist to a room of stark simplicity.

The classical vocabulary of ornament also played a pivotal role. Acanthus leaves, rams' heads, scrolls, rosettes, and flower garlands were but a few examples of decorative motifs that brought the flavor of antiquity to a mirror frame, a candlestick, or a clock. To this could be added other artifacts in the simple, geometric forms related to the architectural principles of antiquity—cube, sphere, arch, and triangle—forms that echoed the tenor of the past, yet would not be out of place in a modern interior.

ROOMS

The guileless, restrained dimension of simpler neoclassical style found favor on both sides of the Atlantic for interior decoration. Its exponents realized that decorating in the neoclassical taste need not rely on the eloquent simplicity characteristic of the designs of Robert Adam, nor upon the flamboyant and highly stylized opulence that had been created for Napoleon by the French architects Percier and Fontaine in the early nineteenth century. The simple neoclassical style is unpretentious, giving a nod to the principles that defined the antique past, yet at the same time refusing to be drawn into Thomas Hope's battle for a rigid adherence to authenticity.

A room decorated in a simple neoclassical style is extremely satisfying and comfortable in many ways. For example, while drawing inspiration from classical antiquity, it does not attempt to re-create the heavy, florid formality characteristic of a French Empire or English Regency interior. The standards of tranquility and purity that informed the architecture, sculpture, and decoration of classical antiquity

ABOVE In the comfortable library of this 1870s house, a dominant classical bust presides against the neutral sponged wall effect. The collections of bones, skulls, and fossils are reminiscent of a nineteenth-century naturalist cabinet of curiosities.

LEFT This room was the original Federal church built in 1808 in Catskill, New York. The higher level was the area for the Sunday school. Frank Faulkner used his collections of furniture, lighting, paintings, and books to create an exciting environment. He feels there is a sense of rhythm and cadence when you walk into a classical room. The room itself gives you direction, tells you which way to move.

are especially at home in a simple neoclassical room, in a way that could perhaps be said to draw parallels with Japanese culture and taste. Both look to tradition to enlighten, and take inspiration from the essence of what is beautiful and pure, but they do not strive slavishly to imitate it exactly. Because it lacks pretension and does not appear self-conscious, the simple neoclassical style celebrates what is beautiful, classic, and natural.

Entering a room decorated in a simple version of the neoclassical style does not immediately conjure images of the antique past. The overall effect is rather more subtle, evoking the spirit of the classical past by making allusion to it. These artful references might take the form of a motif of palmettes, acanthus leaves, or garlands that ornament a mirror frame, for example, a door surround with the simple lines of a Greek temple, or a floor that has been gridded to resemble limestone.

An interior decorated in the simple neoclassical style looks to the ancient Greek and Roman past to create an atmosphere that is fundamentally spare and uncomplicated, but which enchants with a decorative vocabulary boasting rich and sumptuous details. Windows are without curtains in order to maximize light. Against a backdrop of floors made of marble, stripped pine, or oak, and walls composed of roughly worked stucco or sponged with a pale color are placed furnishings and decorative ornaments that are deliberate quotations from classical antiquity. A Corinthian column serving as a pedestal for a modern sculpture, a bronze vase forming the base of a lamp, or a table that boasts a Medici-style urn as a support—these are modest but decorative references to the classical past. At the heart of a simple neoclassical interior remain the enduring principles of symmetry, clarity, and form.

LEFT, TOP This elegant dining room, with its stripped floorboards painted to resemble stone and monochromatic scheme, allows for maximum utilization of light. There are no curtains: the eighteenth-century house is used like a lantern. The main features are sepia prints, nineteenth-century balloon-back chairs, and a classic table painted white.

LEFT, CENTER In this Germantown New York, house from the 1870s, nothing is quite as it seems. The dining-room floor has been sponged and divided into a grid to look like limestone. The *faux*-granite table is medium-density fiberboard resting on a garden urn. The Queen-Anne-style chairs are painted an uncharacteristic bright white to contrast with the sponged coral walls.

LEFT, BOTTOM The designer Andrea Truglio has created a retreat of restrained classicism in his nineteenth-century apartment in the center of Rome. The elements of architectural details, the columns and moldings, have been carefully designed to give strong shape but no decoration. They lead the eye to the room beyond.

RIGHT The walls of this elegant living area in Frank Faulkner's house in Catskill, New York, have retained the raw plaster. Frank could not paint it since he loves the Chardin tones. The chairs were bought secondhand and then covered in white loose covers. They surround a Charles X mahogany table.

DECORATIVE

EVERY CENTURY HAS DEPENDED on decoration to bring a sense of comfort, warmth, and individuality to the home interior, be it through the decorative detail of the rooms themselves or the objects gathered within them. Decorative styles draw inspiration from a variety of divergent ornamental traditions, from the pure classicism of the Italian Renaissance to the folk crafts and rural influences of colonial America or Scandinavia. Inspiration also came from the exotic conventions of cultures as diverse as the indigenous arts of North Africa, China, Japan, India, and Mexico, whose impact increased with the marked growth in overseas trade and contact from the nineteenth century onward. Along with these cross-cultural influences, color also plays a pivotal role. Highly creative, the decorative embraces what is eclectic, borrowing any number of references from uniquely individual styles and then mixing them to great effect.

One of the most traditional ways to decorate an interior is to tell a story on its walls. As an original focus for a room, painted walls lend a background of warmth and comfort. Whether they depict a rural view of animals grazing or surrounding architectural splendor reminiscent of a grand Roman villa, they have the power to conjure up a unique sense of theater for all kinds of interiors.

STORIES ON WALLS

The practice of decorating walls with narrative scenes has roots in the classical past, when the tombs of the ancient Etruscans and Egyptians were painted with lively and colorful stories celebrating the life of departed loved ones. Scenes of domestic life, feasts and banquets, musical parties, hunting, and parades were favorite themes for the wall decorations of these burial chambers. In the grand villas of sophisticated ancient cities such as Rome and Pompeii, frescoed walls illustrating landscapes, theater scenes, and mythology delighted the wealthy proprietors and their guests.

In the Middle Ages in Europe, wall paintings, like most other aspects of decoration, were heavily religious in their themes, as preserved in churches and monasteries. Secular themes were also taken up, although surviving examples are relatively few. With the flowering of the Renaissance, painted walls found a ready place again, not only in churches, but also in the palaces and homes of the nobility, as illustrated by the numerous frescoes by the leading artists of southern Europe. This period set an example for ages to come in its variety of subjects and techniques of mural painting. Leonardo, Michelangelo, and Raphael, among others, painted frescoes that set standards not only for wall painting, but also for the development of figured art overall.

As the fresco technique diminished in popularity and painters turned increasingly to canvas and other media, wall painting reverted more to decorative motifs, turning away from highly sophisticated figural subjects. Yet the Old Masters were instrumental in incorporating decorative motifs into their works and passing them down in various guises to later craftsmen. The *grotteschi*, or "grotesques," of Raphael represent just such an example. Even today, these motifs are happily incorporated into modern mural paintings.

OPPOSITE: TOP LEFT In the New York house of Juan Pablo Molyneux, "grotesques" are painted on canvas, and the floor is painted to simulate elaborate parquet. While including strange and uncommon animals, these paintings also make reference to the family and its pets.

TOP RIGHT The Renaissance decoration in this London kitchen was inspired by the Mappa Mundi room in Rome's Palazzo Sacchetti. Here the frescoes are adapted to a small eighteenth-century house.

BOTTOM LEFT Artist Johannes Larsen's dining room in Funen, Denmark, is representative of local early-twentieth-century painting. Its bird scene is painted as if there are no walls, with local images: Kerteminde landscapes, Hverringe coastline, and Lundsgaard cliff.

BOTTOM RIGHT The dining room in this house in Columbia County, New York, has been painted in naïve Hudson River style by Robert Jackson. Its wall painting includes scenes from the county and even a portrait of the house.

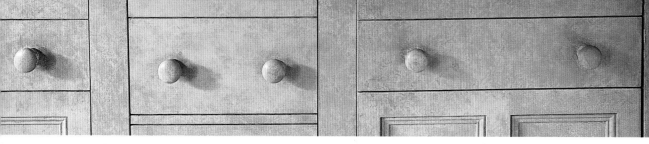

LEFT The unusual painted decoration in the kitchen of the same London house shown on page 67 was also inspired by the Mappa Mundi room in the Palazzo Sacchetti. In this low-ceilinged room, the pillars and figures seem to support the top, giving the illusion of a double-height space.

BELOW LEFT In the same townhouse, innovative use of color and pattern adorn the bath, walls, ceiling, washbasin surround, and cabinet. By use of light and shade, the artist has created a three-dimensional effect.

EARLY ITALIAN TRADITION

Picturesque frescoes adorned the walls of Roman villas, and these were to exert particular influence over artists of the Italian Renaissance and beyond. The archaeological discoveries of Pompeii and Herculaneum unearthed four styles of painting that furnished a fertile vocabulary of material and inspiration for the various "Pompeiian" phases of eighteenth- and nineteenth-century interior design. They comprised murals depicting open landscape vistas, creating the sense of looking out of a window; figure scenes; walls painted to resemble different marble or with illusionistic

architectural features, such as columns and pilasters; and patterns of pictures painted as if they were hanging on the wall. Today these kinds of age-old ornamental details make a striking backdrop and original decorative scheme in a modern interior.

The discovery of ancient Roman painted decorations, such as those excavated in the Golden House of Nero in Rome, brought to light intricate, delicate wall decorations buried for centuries in subterranean ruins and grottoes. These patterns, which came to be known as "grotesques," were comprised of loosely connected motifs similar to arabesques, but with the addition of human figures, monkeys, and sphinxes. A number of early Renaissance artists adopted individual motifs from the recently discovered grotesques, but it was Raphael who

RIGHT AND BELOW
These high-quality painted "grotesques" are known as *singerie*, from the French word for monkey. This style of decoration, developed in the seventeenth and eighteenth centuries, consisted of monkey figures usually frolicking and mimicking human habits and pastimes, in scrolling foliage and light bandwork. J. Berain produced famous designs for *singeries*. This lighter decorative touch heralded the early Rococo designs. The cornice has been made from specially commissioned classical emblems by Juan Pablo Molyneux.

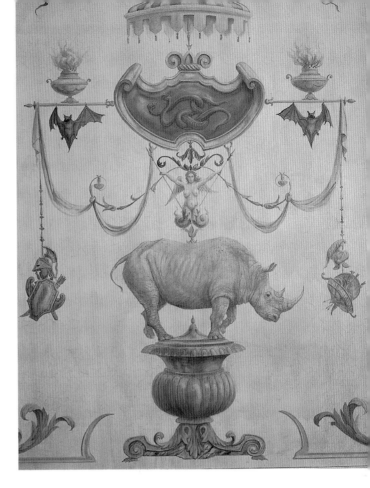

first revived them as a complete decorative scheme for walls in the Vatican Logge, in the form of narrow panels. Engravings disseminated the designs throughout Europe, and they remain popular today for wall and ceiling decoration, painted panels, and tapestries.

FOLK TRADITION

The concept of stories on walls also has roots in the rural tradition: over the centuries, itinerant folk painters would travel through the countryside seeking employment. Inspired by their surroundings, many of these painters

ABOVE AND LEFT The dining room in this Dutch house in Columbia County, New York, originally built around 1730, has recently been decorated with naïve Hudson River painting by Robert Jackson. Pamela Kline chose all her favorite naïve paintings to be copied, such as work by Ammi Phillips (1788–1865) and Charles C. Hofmann (1821–1882). The colors used are traditional, and most of the paints are Colonial Williamsburg.

brought into the interior the beauty of nature and the landscape by painting vivid scenes of country life. A farmer plowing his fields, sheep and cows grazing, peasants harvesting, and a variety of birds, ducks and geese—a panorama that is a constant reminder of familiar and comforting aspects of the home, and a virtual window from which to view the pleasures of the outdoors. Wall paintings depicting flowers, fruit, and trees were other favorite ways of bringing the delights of the garden inside the house. In wealthier households the walls were frequently

ABOVE AND RIGHT The dining room in the Johannes Larsen house in Kerteminde, Denmark, was painted in the Funen style in 1916, with typical rural inspirations. The artists were less interested in ornithology than in bird forms and colors. The red used was a Chinese pigment called "zinober." These walls were decorated with fresco painting and were meant to bring all the artists' favorite landscape and nature scenes inside. The Danes love color and, in common with many northern peoples, use bright hues to cheer up the long winter nights.

COLORS
The palette for folk decoration often reflects the colors of the surrounding countryside: the green of the fields and trees, the blue of the sky and sea, and the reddish terracotta and sienna of the earth. The style was also influenced by colors used by itinerant painters and could therefore embrace hues from far-off lands.

engravings on walls was enthusiastically taken up for more modest surroundings. Entire rooms were decorated with prints pasted directly onto papered or painted walls and even doors. Initially popular in England, Ireland, and France, this trend for print rooms also took hold on the other side of the Atlantic Ocean, especially in grander houses in the southern states. Oftentimes, black-and-white prints with black borders were simply pasted on straw-colored walls in regimented rows. More theatrical arrangements, including those devised by Robert Adam and Thomas Chippendale, employed trompe l'oeil paper cutouts of classical swags, bows, garlands, and chains that appeared to support prints "hanging" on the walls.

The nineteenth-century Empire style in France lent itself to the grandeur of mural painting, with peaceful, pastoral scenes recalling the eighteenth-century *fêtes galantes* or rural gatherings depicted in the paintings of Watteau and Lancret. This tradition of pastoral murals has carried through to the present, reflecting over the years the various abstract and minimalist currents in painting of the day.

ABOVE AND RIGHT These frescoes in the hallway of a seventeenth- and eighteenth-century manor house in the Dordogne region of southwestern France were painted in 1911, probably by someone in the family who owned the house. They are not of quite the same quality as other frescoes in the house but are historically interesting, with images of airplanes and people playing badminton. The *enfilade* (a piece of furniture for a corridor) was painted to echo the walls. The stairs are in unusual Chinese Chippendale style, and the under-dado is typically marbled in a rustic style. The wall finish is color-washed to keep a more rural appearance.

embellished with elaborate decorative schemes, with painters employed to decorate walls so that they appeared to be hung with framed paintings, for example.

In the eighteenth and nineteenth centuries there emerged a fashion for decorating walls with paintings of classical ruins and architectural studies of Grand Tour sites, or with scenes from Greek and Roman mythology. Although less expensive oil paintings were primarily confined to the grand houses belonging to the aristocracy, the less expensive and perfectly acceptable convention of collecting and hanging framed prints and

ABOVE An itinerant painter decorated most of this Dordogne manor house's hallway in 1876. These painters traveled the countryside and would stay with the owners until the task was completed. Romantic outdoor pursuits were particularly popular subjects for such artists in the late nineteenth century. The green wicker bench was made in England, and the chateau birdcage in France, both toward the end of the nineteenth century.

By definition, the eclectic interior borrows from a wide variety of sources to create its own style. At the heart of the artistic doctrine of eclecticism lies the notion that examples of excellence from any great styles—even if they seem mutually incompatible—can be combined to create something of great beauty. More everyday pieces may also be brought together successfully if they are chosen with confidence and panache.

ECLECTICISM

The eclectic interior is singled out from other styles of decoration by its lack of rules. There is no right or wrong way to put things together, although admittedly certain combinations may jar the sensibilities or be unpleasing to the eye. But it remains a highly personal style, and therein lies its strength. It can be witty and dramatic, spirited and sensuous, eccentric, adventurous and colorful, or a combination of these qualities. What it is not is dull, but rather a highly original way of creating surroundings that reflect an appreciation for the beauty of other cultures and other times.

At its least successful, eclecticism can seem nothing more than a confusing mishmash of furnishings or objects that have nothing to do with each other and create an ambience of clutter and chaos. At its best, however, when pieces are chosen with care and combined with skill, it demonstrates the kind of beauty and harmony that can be found among related kinds of objects, similar shapes or colors that marry well. Above all, it champions the unique, the interesting, and the unusual.

Eclectic taste reached its apex in Victorian times, embracing a variety of input from different cultures and eras: Renaissance, eighteenth-century French Rococo, Elizabethan, and Gothic were among the fashionable styles that seized the popular imagination on both sides of the Atlantic. Add to this mix of styles the fact that empires were expanding and doors were opening to an increase in trade and travel, and the result was that a great variety of furniture and artifacts from distant cultures was given pride of place in the decoration of interiors. Happily, eclecticism remains alive and well in the twenty-first century; it tends, however, to take a subtler form—not so much gatherings of disparate objects but themed collections and cross-fertilization between styles and traditions.

OPPOSITE: TOP LEFT The secret of eclecticism is strong statement and the combination of interesting objects. They can be from any artistic tradition and any period. This is not a style for the fainthearted.

TOP RIGHT The strong red of the walls, the bronze busts, and the watercolors of European scenes exhibited on this wall and door all show the collector's enthusiasm.

BOTTOM LEFT A wonderful display of Victorian exuberance in decorative art and nature study. This nature tableau consists of elaborate porcelain flowers, shell vases and paperweights, some as sand specimens formed into views of the Isle of Wight. The backdrop is floral wallpaper.

BOTTOM RIGHT A collection of Whitefriars and Walsh straw opaline glass from the late nineteenth century needs to be properly lit and set against red velvet to show its distinctive colors.

COLOR AND PATTERN

The eclectic interior has no fear of color, embracing the entire spectrum with enthusiasm. Its colors do not jar, but complement each other in fresh and exciting ways. A wall may be equally effective as a vibrant part of a collection or as a self-effacing backdrop; wall paneling painted in the traditional shades of pale creams or white detailed with bold strokes of a strong hue brings a room to life, while bold geometric designs—diamond-patterned tiles, the arrangement of pictures on a wall—jump out from subtle, pale-colored backgrounds.

Colors and patterns are mixed together in a dizzying array of permutations, arresting the eye here and there. A plain piece of furniture or an expanse of wall space can be enlivened through the use of vividly contrasting colors, as well as by the arrangement of engaging patterns of decorative artifacts. Furniture and objects both ornamental and functional form an integral part of the decorative scheme: a kitchen cabinet displays colorful china plates, shelves heaving

LEFT In the Kerteminde area of Denmark, many doors within houses are painted in off-white/cream gloss with dark brownish-red detailing. This color is often called "bull's blood." It creates a very dramatic backdrop in the "coffee kitchen," where the family could make coffee or tea when the maids had gone home. The eye is led on by the vibrant blue beyond.

BELOW LEFT This bedroom has quite simple late-nineteenth-century mahogany furniture. Interest is created by the bright blue on the walls, some large paintings by Alhed Larsen, and a series of prints from Fritz Syberg's illustrations to Hans Christian Andersen's *A Mother*.

BELOW The joy of color is essential to a Dane, particularly an artist such as Johannes Larsen. This vermilion on the walls was considered an excellent counterpoint to the art of the Funen painters. The doors of the house were painted with eleven coats of paint when the house was built and have not been painted since.

LEFT The bright red on the walls of the Larsen house shows off the wonderful portraits and landscapes of the Funen painters. They were scorned by art critics, who described them as "the peasant painters." The late-nineteenth-century table, chairs, and sofa were wedding gifts to Johannes and Alhed Larsen.

BELOW This wall color reflects the group of 1870s Minton porcelain pieces, in the Japanese taste, some designed by Christopher Dresser. The cabinet, which is typical of the Aesthetic style, was designed by Charles Bevan. This is an example of a collection that has been dictated by a factory, a style, a type of decoration, and even a color.

COLORS Here, to be bold is not a suggestion, but an instruction. The effect can be achieved with pale colors covered with multicolored, multi-textured objects or by using vibrant colors that attack the senses. Vivid reds, dazzling blues, moody greens, and glorious yellows—the eclectic palette is just that. An important aspect to this style is how room leads into room and color leads on to color, all chosen to stimulate and excite.

with rows of books surrounded by paintings decorate a wall, or a thoughtfully arranged corner cupboard holds a treasured collection of sculpture and ceramics. The well-considered, skillful positioning of such objects within an interior can create the impression of a decorative pattern.

Light on dark, dark on light—colors can be juxtaposed in endless varieties in an eclectic interior. Colors and patterns run riot across walls, floors, and ceilings. At the same time, they contribute to the whole. When well combined, they imbue an interior with a sense of both mischief and orderliness. Clever mixtures of contrasting colors and motifs result in a highly original decorative style brimming with imagination and confidence.

ARTIFACTS

One of the joys of the eclectic interior is its unrelenting ability to surprise and delight continuously. Bringing together artifacts from different cultures or eras and combining them in imaginative and unusual ways can bring a room to life, while challenging time-honored notions of decorating styles.

Beginning in the Italian Renaissance, the world opened up to exploration, and connoisseurs everywhere created "cabinets of curiosities" for their collections of unusual, exotic objects. Coins and medals, vessels made from precious materials such as rock crystal, rare jewels, sumptuous silks, and porcelain and lacquer from the East were among the exquisite treasures that were assembled and admired by a chosen few. This practice, which came into its own in the second half of the nineteenth century, has hardly changed over the centuries, but in the modern world the pleasure and

ABOVE Mirrors can double the joy of collecting. Here reflected is a central *electrolier* by W. A. S. Benson (a contemporary of William Morris), along with Doulton china, a Martinware bird, and other glimpses of porcelain and watercolors. On the mantelpiece, two bronzes— "Perseus Holding the Head of Medusa" by Pomeroy and "The Sluggard" by Lord Leighton— flank a nineteenth-century clock of three faces, telling time, day, and month; weather; and moon.

LEFT You either love it or you hate it: taxidermy is a great favorite of the eclectic collector. In this room a pair of nineteenth-century cupboards provide a suitable nesting spot, as does a Chinese chest. These stuffed birds seem quite at home in a light, bright Victorian environment.

satisfaction of collecting unusual objects lies not only in owning a cabinet of curiosities, but also in living with them every day.

Artifacts assembled from around the world —such as ivory or wooden carvings, glass vessels or ceramic plates, and lavish textiles or furniture made from unusual materials such as bamboo or lacquer—stand side by side with collections of flora and fauna specimens in a twenty-first-century eclectic interior. Especially at home are handcrafted articles, for instance, pottery or folk paintings. Considerable appeal lies in decorating with objects that were not originally intended for decoration but created for more practical purposes. Objects from different periods in time are also combined to great effect, in keeping with the eclectic approach to decorating that emerged during the high Victorian era.

The success of an interior decorated with an eclectic mixture of artifacts is largely determined by the way they work together, either creating a cohesive space or grouped so as to shock; either way, a strong sense of purpose and aesthetic vision are required. While pure quality alone can sometimes be enough to justify the role accorded to a piece, more often objects of similar shape, material, color, or function work cooperatively together to create a unified, decorative yet comfortable backdrop for living. A similar effect may be achieved by items tied together by a thematic connection— for instance, contemporary versions of historical originals, such as pottery that draws inspiration from ancient Greek vase painting.

Eclecticism is always a highly personal style. What ultimately defines the character of an eclectic interior is the use of decorative objects that celebrate the unusual, the unfamiliar, and perhaps even the exotic, brought together with a touch of imagination and flair.

ABOVE From the bright blue Wedgwood "Portland" vase to the classically inspired vases, ewers, and pots, nineteenth-century pieces like these drew inspiration from the ancient Greeks, Romans, Egyptians, and Etruscans. The common themes bring a visual unity.

FURNITURE

An interior furnished in eclectic style exalts in freedom from the constraints of adherence to any particular historically correct style. In the late nineteenth century, the growing middle classes, who sought to emulate fashion but generally lacked the confidence or inclination to decorate in forward-looking modern taste, found comfort in traditions of the past. The result was furniture that looked to a variety of historical periods for inspiration—Renaissance, Gothic, Elizabethan, French Baroque, Rococo, and neoclassical—at times combining features from several styles. These pieces might be constructed with indigenous woods that would not have been used for the originals. Although looking back to the past, they were inevitably new, highly imaginative versions of time-honored furniture designs. One of the most innovative designers was the Austrian cabinetmaker François Linke; working in Paris, he developed a signature style that mixed the traditions of Louis XV with Art Nouveau.

Materials for decoration were also subject to experiments. These focused on age-old decorative techniques: inlays of ivory, ebony, and mother-of-pearl; marquetry veneers using rare and precious woods; tortoiseshell and metals such as pewter and brass; as well as straightforward painting and parcel gilding.

Modern eclectic furniture is similarly patterned on traditional designs, with freedom to experiment. An English Regency drum table, for example, is rendered in brass with decorative touches unknown in the nineteenth century. The eclectic potpourri of styles and materials allows furniture crafted for one purpose to take on new life through use in another context.

ABOVE It takes a bold collector to want her culinary efforts overseen by a stuffed aviary and the fish that got away. However, since the late-nineteenth-century tables and chairs were made in the golden period of taxidermy, everything seems to fit rather well.

RIGHT, ABOVE The Aesthetic Movement was certainly not about minimalism. The allover floral-pattern wallpaper, paintings, fire screen, and Victorian inlaid papier-mâché chair, combined with a vibrantly colored Persian rug, create an exotic ambiance.

RIGHT, BELOW In this artist's studio in Denmark, the paintings, whether landscape, portrait, or still life, are all set in the local countryside. The constant desire to bring the outside in is here seen in the ceiling painting of birds in flight on a summer day.

ROOMS

Interiors decorated with an eye to eclecticism embrace a style that has brought together a variety of very different cultural influences. Favorite historical themes look to the Italian Renaissance, the Gothic, eighteenth-century French Rococo, and classicism, with nods to the East and exotic references derived from the civilizations of Africa and Asia.

By the 1880s, eclecticism had emerged as a conspicuous feature of the home interior on both sides of the Atlantic. An overpowering clutter of small decorative objects and pictures fought for attention with richly upholstered seat furniture lavished with cushions and shawls, numerous small tables laden with trinkets and oddities, and a variety of desks, cabinets, and bookcases set against a dark backdrop of heavy curtains, patterned carpets, and dark-colored paintwork, wallpaper, or wall paneling. In what is broadly termed a Victorian interior, a wide

variety of historical styles converged, with each one allocated to a particular room or rooms according to its function. This meant that a pastiche of historical styles—French Rococo, Elizabethan, Gothic, Italian Renaissance, and exotic Moorish designs for furniture, textiles, and decorative objects—typically lived together under one roof.

All art is nourished by tradition, and the modern interior furnished in that same spirit of eclecticism has moved beyond the somewhat confused assemblage of revival styles that characterized the Victorian interior to become a statement of worldly sophistication and individuality. Unpredictable and imaginative, yet with a sense of order, rooms decorated with an exuberant mix of the traditional and the unusual exude warmth and comfort while pleasing the senses and delighting the eye.

As the world opened up to travelers from the late seventeenth century onward, interior decoration began to draw inspiration from other cultures and traditions. China, India, and Japan, followed by Africa and the Near East, served as fertile spheres of artistic influence. The colorful customs of these remote and distant lands fired the imagination and opened new paths of understanding and artistic appreciation.

EXOTIC

The exotic East has long provided inspiration for interiors. In the late seventeenth to eighteenth centuries, the appeal of furniture and artifacts from India, China, and Japan, brought to Europe via the voyages of the East India Companies, exercised enormous influence on fashionable taste. Originating from an aesthetic entirely at odds with the art of the West, objects and furnishings of exotic materials—lacquer, porcelain, and sumptuous silks—were among the imported treasures from India and the Orient that captured the European imagination.

Over time, European craftsmen developed a style that emulated the furnishings from the East and became known as chinoiserie, while Oriental artisans began to modify their wares to incorporate the idiosyncrasies of European fashions. In the late 1870s, a particularly British decorative style emerged, based on the art of Japan. Called the Aesthetic Movement, it championed the philosophy that beauty was far more important for living than any kind of practical considerations.

Perhaps more than any other style, the exotic is laden with showy colors and dazzling, out-of-the-ordinary materials, and it opens the door to what stimulates, excites, and inspires the imagination. It is a way of decorating that pays tribute to the theatrical. And because it is not hidebound to conventional ideas of taste and formulaic decorative styles, it recognizes what is beautiful in simple folk crafts as well as in sophisticated, self-possessed furnishing and artifacts.

A brightly colored tribal mask made from braided reeds and papier-mâché; a lacquer cabinet placed on a gilded, richly carved stand; or a floor covering made from zebra hide—such pieces are at home in a room that invites in the exotic. Whatever it is combined with, the exotic interior charts its own path; worldly, sophisticated, and erudite, it is a fearless style.

OPPOSITE: TOP LEFT Influence from the East does not always have to be colorful and unusual. In a Japanese-style bedroom seen through *shoji* paper-screen doors, serenity, simplicity, and soft natural colors create total calm.

TOP RIGHT African carvings and masks immediately hint at an exotic and exuberant culture.

BOTTOM LEFT A mountain goat's head on an Indian silvered metal chair has a distinctly Assyrian quality. The shape and embossed metalwork are unquestionably Eastern.

BOTTOM RIGHT An atmosphere of the Orient can be created by strong images. These two carved wooden figures of Buddha instantly bring an air of serenity to a room, particularly set off against the white walls.

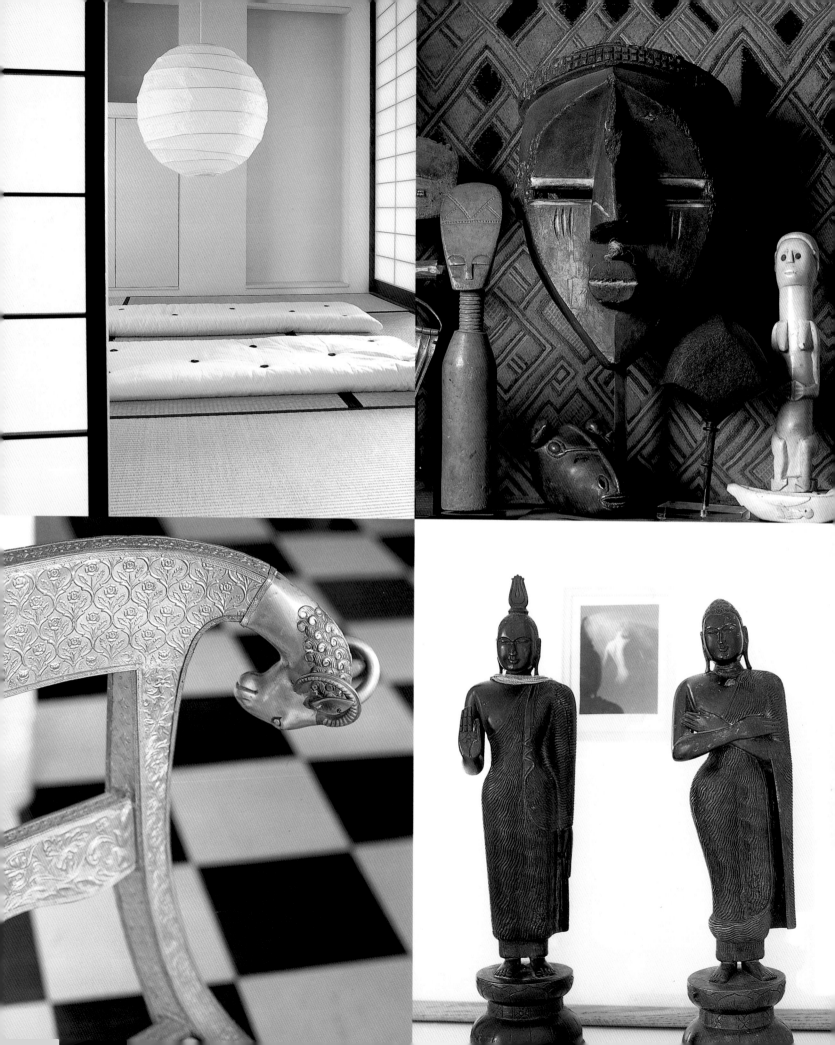

COLOR

Exotic styles allow a broad spectrum of colors, both rich and pale. Used with a combination of courage and restraint, they imbue an interior with the spirit of another world.

The color palette of the East is at once confident and subdued. Vibrant greens, blues, yellow, black, and, most importantly, the seductive shade of scarlet are among the colors that frequently spring to mind in relation to China, while cool, pale tones—white, light greens, blues, yellows, and coral—reflect the tranquility and serenity associated with Japan.

ABOVE Even without the Chinese calligraphy, this room exudes an aura of China due to Sonja Caproni's combination of vermilion, black, and white.

ABOVE RIGHT The natural materials and soft colors of this Japanese-style room, with sliding *shoji* paper screens and fine *tatami* matting, provide the option of the space being used for dining, sleeping, or just relaxing in the serene atmosphere.

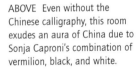

COLORS The Western world's obsession with all things exotic can be displayed in the color palette. From the neutrals of Japan and China to exotic Imperial Ming Gold (yellow), vivid greens, and vibrant vermilion, from the natural patina of wood to deep, luxurious ebony and scorching tribal reds, everything is available to calm or excite the senses.

壺乾堪式

ABOVE A few clever additions can create that distinctly Oriental feel. The ancient Chinese sign, the aged green paint, the sofa with bamboo legs, and the patterned silk lamps take us from Spitalfields in London to the back streets of Shanghai.

LEFT The natural color of these woven African pots with their distinctive geometric designs is enhanced by the use of terracotta paint behind. The bright red ceremonial tribal hats hanging above further enhance the scene.

But eye-catching brights are also found in the Japanese spectrum, and the pure pale colors of jades and *blanc-de-chine* porcelain vessels contradict the notion that the Chinese only honor what is flashy and bold.

Many of these colors are reflected in the handcrafted objects that are synonymous with these cultures—the pale celadon green of Chinese porcelain, the bright inky blue and vivid red of Japanese Imari porcelain ware, or the lustrous black highlighted with gold of a lacquer screen. Textiles and woodblock prints also offer a range of hues that together work to summon up the mood of quiet self-assurance and restraint that underlies the ideology of the exotic East.

Alternatively, against the backdrop of the hot, sultry climates and scorched earth of Africa, India, and the Near East springs another range of colors that may also equip an interior with a bizarre, exotic flavor. Vibrant hues typical of the vivid cotton prints of African fabrics—bright greens, intense yellows, fiery vermilion, and blue—crash together in riotous combinations, tempered by the pale, dry shades—light terracottas, buffs, and softer yellows—that echo with the warm dust of an arid, sand-colored desert landscape. These colors also marry well with the pinks and golds of a silken Indian sari. Whether subtly combined or boldly solo, they are part of the aura of elsewhere.

RIGHT, FROM TOP Leopard-print fabric on a daybed from a hotel in Casablanca is exotic and authentic. It was a popular covering for chairs and sofas, particularly in the French Empire style.

A nineteenth-century Chinese wedding cupboard with the edge of an eighteenth-century gilt-wood French chair in a contemporary London loft. The square of gray behind the cupboard brings a sense of unity and fusion.

An eighteenth-century Damascus chest with mother-of-pearl inlay provides historical perspective to modern ceramics and a painting by Althea Wilson. Many of her ceramics are based on shapes of large Chinese rhubarb leaves.

OPPOSITE, FROM TOP A Chinese table sits in the hallway of a Columbia County house in New York built in 1780. These tables were eagerly imported into America and Europe from the eighteenth century onward.

This lacquer cabinet was in the collection of the Grand Dukes of Baden. It was made in Germany at the beginning of the eighteenth century, when influence from the East was evident in furniture and ceramics.

Although all the ceramics and bronzes, as well as the carved wooden head are German, they sit on a nineteenth-century Chinese apothecary's cabinet.

FURNITURE

In an exotic interior, objects or furnishings from other cultures are often used in new and imaginative ways, for purposes entirely different from their original intent. A wooden marriage chest from India is both decorative and useful as a table, for instance. A Chinese bronze funerary bowl becomes a home for exotic plants. A wooden apothecary's cabinet crafted in Morocco is at once ornamental and functional, providing volumes of storage space.

Since the nineteenth century, Japanese design has influenced Western furniture makers, especially in Britain. Edward Godwin was one of the first to use ebonized wood, lacquer panels, and decorative carved fretwork for his furniture. Another popular furniture material from the Orient was bamboo. During the 1880s and 1890s, North Africa and the Near East also offered inspiration: decorative Moorish chairs, folding screens, occasional tables, and divans piled with cushions and lavishly draped with Turkish carpets or other Near Eastern textiles. And from India evolved portable "campaign" furniture of cots and writing desks, as well as wicker chairs and sofas, planters' chairs, cane blinds, ornate silvered metal furniture, and pieces decorated with ivory carving or black lacquer inlays.

Modern versions of these designs continue to bring a fresh, exotic flavor to interiors today, as do traditional furnishings from China and Japan. The spare, geometric forms and reliance on lacquer finishes or inlays of exotic materials fit neatly with contemporary furniture or with styles from other periods.

Unconventional use of materials and fabrics also contributes to color and exotic spice. Leather used to cover a door, for example, bold animal prints on chairs, mirror glass as a table top, or cushions woven with bamboo—such surprising and imaginative twists add vitality.

BELOW Sonja Caproni has taken this rather dark space in a New York apartment and created a dining room with character and hints of the exotic. The mirrored walls, applied columns, and leather-finished doors afford light and depth. The most dominant focus in the room is the 1940s chairs —designed by Frances Elkins, who was inspired by the English architect Edwin Lutyens—which develop the exotic theme.

ARTIFACTS

The eye that takes pleasure in the exotic looks beyond convention to find beauty in unusual objects. Tribal art, hugely varied in form and style, embodies a different aesthetic from the art of the West, and many artifacts chosen to decorate an exotic room dazzle with their originality and inventiveness, bringing a sense of theater and spectacle. The perfection of an ancient Greek statue would be out of place in an exotic interior; the beauty and vitality in a primitive, naïve carving of a wooden idol from Africa lies not in perfection, but in an expression that celebrates the anomalies of the human form.

Fundamental to a space decorated in the spirit of the exotic are unusual materials and textures indigenous to a particular land. Wood, bronze, lacquer, pottery and porcelain, marble and stone, as well as animal skins and fabrics woven from natural materials such as cane, straw or bamboo, cotton, linen, and silks—all will find a place in the exotic interior. Imagination plays an important role in making native artifacts decorative in the modern interior, as it figures in the way objects are combined and displayed.

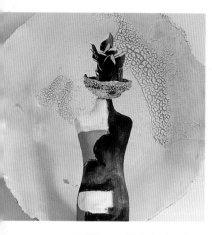

ABOVE On a Victorian fireplace in London, a modern stoneware dummy by Althea Wilson adds an exotic touch.

BELOW Hubert Zander uses his collection of tribal artifacts, centered on the wonderful tribal hat, to make a visual statement in a very small hallway. This eclectic mix of tribal art, taxidermy, and books creates a real "explorer" feel.

The panoply of objects includes many created for specific uses. African tribal carvings in wood or antique ivory, as well as tribal masks, spears, and shields, are artifacts intended for religious, warlike, or ceremonial rituals. Collections of objects from a particular culture, be it India, China, or Africa, whose function is embedded in tradition—Japanese dress accessories such as *inro* medicine cases or *netsuke* toggles, for example— add interest and flavor. Among the artifacts at home in an exotic interior are mountings for swords or armor, gaming pieces, food and writing boxes, ink paintings, burial vessels, lanterns, and incense burners. The cross-cultural mix of remote source and fresh eye is key.

LEFT These Ebegi dolls were made by the Yoruba tribe in Nigeria. If a mother gave birth to twins and they died, the mother would look after the dolls as if they were her children, washing and feeding them. Such emotive tribal art carvings influenced Picasso.

RIGHT A collection of African masks is grouped carefully as if they are taking part in some hidden ritual. Artifacts from different cultures fascinate us, adding mystery and sometimes a certain amount of unease. They visually dominate their surroundings.

LEFT The secret of displaying collections is to create a visual conversation piece. Here Chinese lanterns sit on one table, while amusing Oriental figures chase each other around another.

RIGHT Althea Wilson's painting, with glorious shades of yellow, throws focus on a Benin bronze cast of the head of a queen.

RIGHT Japanese style sits happily with contemporary architecture in this London loft-style apartment. The Oriental sofa, chairs, and low table are arranged traditionally in front of the enormous windows overlooking the River Thames. The color of the upholstery adds warmth to the walls of textured render and floor tiles of slate.

BELOW In a New York apartment Sonja Caproni has taken a very neutral setting and created a striking Oriental scene. This has been achieved with the black lacquered furniture, massive Chinese pots, and cast "branch" lights with moonstones and rock crystal pinned to the stem to look like barnacles.

ABOVE A mixture of styles will create a lively, diverting interior. A lacquer cabinet made in Britain at the time of Charles II sits on an elaborate scroll-leaf and floral stand. The hand-knitted raffia cushions are by Althea Wilson.

RIGHT In the same London townhouse, Althea Wilson has effortlessly blended old and new. Above the Victorian fireplace sits an oil portrait of Charles II next to modern ceramics. The nineteenth-century Burmese carved planter's chair is covered with a zebra rug. On the wall above is an eighteenth-century Venetian mirror. The rugs on the floor are stripped buffalo skin, which looks like paper.

ROOMS

Oriental taste has continued to enjoy favor for interior decoration in the West since it first captured the imagination in the late seventeenth century. Other exotic tastes, inspired by India, North Africa, and beyond, followed hot on its heels. They provide a striking contrast to the traditional Western interior. The spare, tranquil disposition of a room that takes inspiration from a decorative style originating in the Far East, for instance, remains enormously appealing as a refuge from a hectic modern lifestyle. Serene and uncluttered, these interiors tend to be sparsely appointed with simple, streamlined furniture set against a backdrop of pale colors and with a minimum of decorative ornament. Lighting fixtures, wall and window treatments, floor coverings, paintings, and a few decorative details—perhaps ceramic

vases or carved wooden boxes—all come together to highlight the purity and restraint that lie at the heart of this style.

At the opposite end of the spectrum is an imaginatively furnished interior that uses a foreign culture as a starting point, but adds character and life by incorporating a host of different influences. Oriental and African tastes, although very different, can both marry effectively with furniture and decorative artifacts from a variety of historic periods and traditions, and in this way remain eternally modern, at home in today's world. A room that boasts an opulent cabinet made of Oriental lacquer, for example, may effortlessly accommodate a sofa covered in white leather along with an African tribal rug and a modern painting. What makes a successful exotic interior is the way these elements are combined for effect, bringing together disparate shapes, textures, and colors to create a cohesive, comfortable whole.

COUNTRY

COUNTRY STYLE EVOLVED from a tradition of simplicity. Its magic lies in its comfortable absence of self-consciousness and timeless love of craftsmanship, which result in a natural look.

For generations it was, ironically, often the rural poor who created classics of interior design as they searched for comfort and durability. At once decorative and functional, country style is defined by distinctive contrasts and harmonies of colors, furnishings, and textures. These are combined with elements drawn from craft traditions that blend seamlessly and are equally at home in an apartment in Paris or New York or a country cottage in Cornwall or Vermont.

In the late nineteenth century, country became a fashionable style, a reaction against extravagant decoration. The rural interior came not only to show reverence for traditional customs that were disappearing, but also to symbolize an ideal way of life.

Country life is relaxed and informal, a celebration of the pleasures and satisfaction of rural pursuits. In country districts everywhere, styles of interior decoration and furnishings tend to be more informal than those in cities, and urban tastes are transformed into heartier versions of their cosmopolitan counterparts. Especially in larger, grander country houses, these rural styles have an elegance of their own.

GRAND COUNTRY

Unlike city dwellings, country houses have always tended to resist change and defy the capricious whims of fashion. Long after it had fallen from favor in town, for example, wood paneling remained popular for the eighteenth-century country-house interior. Country furniture is inclined to be sturdy, robust, and relatively simply decorated. In a grand country house—where furniture may echo sophisticated styles originally crafted in mahogany or walnut or upholstered with sumptuous fabrics—it was usually adapted in oak or fruitwood, or perhaps painted, reflecting the modesty at the heart of the rural tradition. Textiles are plain or in provincial checks or prints, and decorative touches are spare. But this style is not without elegance or grace; sophistication and simplicity coexist side by side.

Every country boasts its own version of grand country style. In eighteenth-century England, it generally conformed to the principles of symmetry and balance that characterized the urban Regency interior, although the overall feeling was more mellow, more rustic, more lived-in. The architectural style of grand country is frequently dictated by materials available for building and the surrounding environment, interior colors reflecting those of the landscape. A Spanish villa mirrors its exotic North African heritage, with brilliant contrasts of bright colors and bold geometric patterns, while a Scandinavian farmhouse celebrates Gustav III's love affair with French styles, and has painted decoration in the crisp, icy colors of the northern climate. In nineteenth-century America, the plantation houses of the rural south—with languorous porches and large, open rooms painted in cool colors to deflect the heat and furnished with rustic versions of furniture designs by Chippendale and Hepplewhite—set a standard of style that remains popular today.

OPPOSITE: TOP LEFT Against the background of a finely detailed eighteenth-century plaster fire-surround, a small group of Meissen bisque musicians play, beside some wild flowers.

TOP RIGHT A pretty unpainted eighteenth-century French table on terracotta tiles sits in front of under-dado paneling in shades of green, blue, and brown. The bathroom cabinets are old chemists' boxes.

BOTTOM LEFT On an American Queen Anne mahogany highboy, the shell or fan carving denotes the work of a skilled cabinet-maker.

BOTTOM RIGHT Against the faded colors of a rural manor-house hall, an eighteenth-century French chair is upholstered in a copy of a Swedish Gustavian fabric.

ARCHITECTURE

Country style—whether it takes the form of the generous proportions of an Italian stuccoed farmhouse in faded shades of pink or ocher, with high beamed ceilings, thick walls, and glossy expanses of ceramic or marble terraces; a traditional Scandinavian farmhouse, which shares with the pioneering New Englanders and Pennsylvania Dutch of early America a reliance on indigenous woods for roofs, ceiling rafters, and floorboards, and a fondness for rich, deep colors for walls and textiles; or a romantic thatch-roofed English cottage—is framed inside and out by the landscape. Architectural style is generally dictated by the materials available for building and by the agriculture of the region. Buildings depend on the land around them, and appear to spring from their surroundings.

Many interiors decorated in a relatively opulent country style boast spacious rooms with lofty ceilings and large windows. At the same

time, flooring of wooden parquet, stone, brick, or quarry tiles, stone fireplaces, and rough plaster or slatted wooden ceilings add a dramatic rustic flavor.

The Elizabethan practice of lining rooms with pale-colored rectangular hardwood paneling set within a molded framework was taken up in the drawing rooms and dining rooms of grander Georgian-style country dwellings on both sides of the Atlantic, but now painted pale, sunny colors. Other rooms might have limewashed walls of brick or stone or rough plasterwork, and exposed beams, imitating humbler country cottages. Following the English Baroque style of the second half of the seventeenth century, the walls might alternatively feature elaborate plasterwork or pine woodwork painted to resemble marble or a finer wood such as walnut. By the eighteenth

ABOVE In the original kitchen of an eighteenth-century manor house, the ancient thick walls kept the building warm in winter and cool in summer, the terracotta tiles have mellowed with age, and the woodwork is painted in traditional tones.

LEFT The chestnut-beam roof structure is typical of the Périgord region of France and here has been made an integral part of the design of the library.

FAR LEFT The wine room was the original kitchen in this seventeenth-century manor house. The thick walls, small windows, and *gravier* (small stones) on the floor are all typical of houses of this period in the Dordogne area in France.

LEFT This eighteenth-century door has been painted in a traditional blue. Such pine doors were never stripped in the eighteenth and nineteenth centuries: pine was considered an inferior wood, to be painted or wood-grained. The glazed part of the door is backed by early-nineteenth-century toile.

RIGHT, ABOVE This carved chestnut fire-surround shows a house of high status. The wide chestnut boards are original to the house, and the unusual banisters on the stair show that the owners in the eighteenth century were aware of design trends from outside the Dordogne.

RIGHT, BELOW In a breakfast room on Long Island, New York, the warm tones of this pine paneling serve as a backdrop to nineteenth-century slat-back or ladderback chairs, an eighteenth-century oak hutch, Chinese export porcelain, and an interesting English Staffordshire blue-and-white tureen, cover, and ladle with a print of the Boston State House.

surface—covered with tongue-and-groove boards rising just above shoulder level and topped with a plate shelf—was painted with a uniform pale hue or coated with colored varnish. Alternatively, the room might boast oak paneling. The fire-surround was seamlessly incorporated into the treatment of the walls, with flooring usually comprised of plain polished boards.

A country-house interior relies on its very architecture to make a decorative statement. A beamed ceiling, the rich honeyed patina of the wall paneling, a strongly defined staircase, a simple window frame or carved overdoor, a brightly colored wooden door, and a stone fireplace—architectural elements such as these at once decorate a room and work together to create a harmonious, sophisticated ambience.

century, the fashion for wood paneling had begun to wane in grander houses, giving way to walls decorated with stucco that were hung with textiles or wallpapered and also embellished with coffered plaster ceilings.

One strand of interior design that has continued to find favor for the grand country house in both Britain and America is the Arts and Crafts style pioneered by William Morris in the second half of the nineteenth century. With an emphasis on handcraftsmanship and traditional techniques using quality native materials, Arts and Crafts artisans produced integrated interior designs that combined the vernacular English with medieval and Eastern themes, alongside plant and animal forms. In keeping with a reverence for the past, wall treatments in Arts and Crafts interiors were faithfully linked with their structure. The fire-surround, for example, played a functional as well as decorative role. In grand country houses decorated in the Arts and Crafts style, the wall

COLOR

Typically, the colors used to decorate the walls of a grand country house reflect the colors of the local landscape. Soft, time-worn colors like thick creams, vanilla, leaf greens, and washed browns are at home in a farmhouse that lives in a cooler climate, while bright whites and deep, vibrant hues abound in regions that enjoy warm weather all year round. Both represent a welcome refuge from the pressures of the urban world.

For rooms decorated in the style of grand country, a light palette consisting of ivory, cream, gray, faded greens, blues, and yellows creates a fitting backdrop for graceful furniture styles and unusual decorative artifacts. Pale colors speak to the simplicity and naturalness that are the essential ingredients of the rural tradition, while at the same time they lend elegance and grandeur to the rustic interior. Walls painted in cool shades of cream, blue, gray, or yellow enhance the lived-in, mellow character of a country farmhouse, as do rooms that boast floors of brick or stone, along with chairs and armoires made of oak or given a coat of paint, distressed to convey the passage of time. Functional objects—ceramics, linens, or

LEFT This main reception room in a house in Claverack, Columbia County, New York was modernized in the Greek Revival style in 1840. The two-tone yellow was a fashionable color of the period and was chosen to reflect the high status of the room.

TOP AND BOTTOM RIGHT In this Périgord *chartreuse* or hunting lodge, many tones of yellow have been used throughout the house. This was a popular color in the area and it also lightens and brightens the rooms.

CENTER RIGHT In an essentially eighteenth-century house in New York State, Farrow and Ball's "Card Room Green" paint has been used.

ABOVE In this bathroom in an eighteenth-century manor house in France, pale tones of yellow and gray-blues have been used. Color-washes give a softer look; flat color can look too modern and harsh in a period room.

OPPOSITE Subtle tones of ocher and yellow color-wash have been used on the walls in this hunting lodge in the Périgord region of France. The Directoire doors have been painted soft gray, and the eighteenth-century French chair has been painted gray-white.

glassware, for instance—that add the all-important decorative touches to a room are also seen at best advantage against a light, sunny background. Especially effective is a combination of various shades of one color, such as yellow, with different shades applied to different sections of walls, thereby creating a soft, luminous impression. In similar fashion, the quiet, clean lines of the Georgian-style furniture favored for a house or apartment in grand country style are complemented by pale colors for walls, floor coverings, and upholstery fabrics, bringing serenity and dignity to the simple and elegant surroundings.

Strong colors, however—rich pinks and crimsons, vibrant greens, daffodil yellow, Prussian blue, and turquoise—are not out of place in the rooms of a grand country house. Bright hues provide the perfect foil for simple,

functional objects, setting off to advantage a single primitive painting, colorful earthenware ceramics, or decorative artifacts such as wooden boxes, woven baskets, or wall lights made of pewter or brass.

Other ways in which bright colors can successfully forge a sense of warmth and comfort in a grander country interior are to be found in the rich hues woven into upholstery textiles. A colorful piece of crewelwork or embroidery, a slice of tapestry, the vivid hues of a provincial quilt, or the imaginative combinations of color found in an Oriental carpet—through items such as these, bright colors make their presence felt. Whether cool and pale or bright or warm, color plays a pivotal role in bringing a cozy and comfortable mood to the rooms of an interior decorated in the grand country style, emphasizing the charms of rural life.

FURNITURE

In England and America, some of the fine furniture of the Georgian and Federal periods found its way into grand country homes. Particularly appropriate to country living are the graceful, restrained Queen Anne and elegant Chippendale styles. As in Britain, mahogany was the favored wood in America, although maple and cherrywood were also popular. The cabinetmaking centers along the eastern seaboard of the United States, from Boston to New York and Philadelphia, produced a variety of distinctive and sophisticated furniture styles that could be at home in both city and country. Comfortable and generously proportioned seat furniture, chests of drawers, beds, secretary-bookcases, tallcase clocks, and tables for tea or gaming—and, unique to America, block-front chests richly carved with large scallop shells—lent dignity and grace to country-house settings.

Along with these fine pieces, however, were many robust and simpler variations on grand furniture that were more appropriate to country life, made locally in the provincial centers.

LEFT In the main salon of a French eighteenth-century manor house near Bordeaux, with its traditional high ceilings, a large eighteenth-century chestnut armoire is flanked by Louis XIV walnut fauteuil chairs. The nineteenth-century armchairs are covered in red denim.

RIGHT A late-nineteenth-century English Arts and Crafts oak sideboard is set against a wall painted in "Amsterdam Green" by Papers and Paints. The mirror is also of the period, as is the large terracotta Joan of Arc that was bought in Paris.

RIGHT, BELOW This early-eighteenth-century side table exudes the quality of a Parisian *ébéniste,* or cabinetmaker. The crispness of the carving and unusual serpentine front would suit the salon of a grand Parisian mansion as well as a grand chateau in the country.

LEFT The Arts and Crafts movement in Britain and America was very much about "fitness for purpose." Function dictated design. Designers turned away from the overdecoration of the late nineteenth century and back to older forms of construction and handcraftsmanship, producing furniture of the style shown.

BELOW The decoration in this salon in a French manor house in the Dordogne region is based on the Elizabethan crewelwork hanging that was the owner's grandmother's. The sophisticated eighteenth-century French cabinet, one of a pair, has its original color.

Taking a cue from the country house of the seventeenth century, furniture in the grand country style is first and foremost comfortable, with roomy chairs—often with matching footstools—and sofas upholstered with turkeywork, velvet, or leather. Oak was eventually replaced by walnut as the fashionable wood, which was often veneered with decorative marquetry patterns, and the taste for exotic Oriental lacquer—for chairs, cabinets, and screens—was also well represented in a grand country setting. High-backed chairs featured scrolled or barley-twist legs and carved

In this master bedroom in a Federal Revival house on Long Island, there are fine examples of American Queen Anne mahogany furniture made during 1725-1750. The style is characterized by delicacy, restrained decoration, and curvilinear forms.

tops, with seats and backs caned or covered in cut velvet or needlework. The all-important bed was fitted with hangings that matched those on the wall, and the new-style dressing tables were embellished with floor-length table coverings or rugs. By the first half of the eighteenth century, mahogany had supplanted walnut for chairs and sofas, dressing and writing tables, chests of drawers, and bureau cabinets, which now boasted the new taste for graceful cabriole legs.

Finely crafted provincial versions that mirror fine urban furniture designs—for example, a Louis XVI-style rush-seated walnut dining chair, a French armoire or curvaceous carved settee in walnut, or a four-poster bed generously appointed with embroidered textile coverlets and hangings—are very much at home in a grand country setting. These relatively rustic examples will happily mix with their more sophisticated cousins, such as an extravagantly carved gilt-wood pier glass, a lavish lacquer cabinet, or a satinwood marquetry tea table. Today the juxtaposition of elegant and sophisticated furnishings with

country-made versions and even forward-looking modern designs creates a sophisticated ambience for the grand country interior. Yet the overall feeling that is ultimately achieved is neither studied nor contrived, but one of great charm, comfort, and relative informality.

In Sweden, the French influence created rural interiors that combined decorativeness with simplicity. Folk furniture is at home in the grandest country-style homes, and the French style did not displace Scandinavian country pieces but rather supplemented them. To the simple rustic furniture, such as traditional three-legged stools and space-saving built-in

ABOVE This nineteenth-century French four-poster bed was painted by artist and specialized decorator Liz Sangster. The colors and finishes are true to the period. The small stool is from Provence and is actually a nineteenth-century nighttime commode.

LEFT A lawyer, John Bay, built a classic Georgian house in Claverack, New York, in 1780. The mahogany tallboy and tripod table were made c.1770. The walls of this hallway are painted with "Biscuit" by Farrow and Ball, and the trim is Stone Colour 3 by Papers and Paints.

FAR LEFT A nineteenth-century naïve painting and distressed painted ladderback (slat-back) chair with a late-eighteenth-century tripod table sit in a late-eighteenth-century hallway.

LEFT The hall of this Long Island home has a mid-eighteenth-century high-style Chippendale longcase clock and an eighteenth-century oak corner chair. These were high-priced items in their day and would have been owned by a man of substance.

benches, beds, and cupboards, were added grander pieces—delicate chairs based on neoclassical shapes popular in France, for instance, such as the Greek *klismos* chair, with its gently swayed back and tapered legs.

Arts and Crafts interiors were best complemented by furniture made of indigenous materials and heavily influenced by vernacular styles. Simple tables, sideboards, and cabinets constructed from traditional hardwoods, such as walnut and oak, relied on the natural figure of the woods for decorative effect or were embellished with pewter, brass, ivory, or leather rather than carved ornamental details. This achieved an effect of solidity and yet, at the same time, elegance. Using traditional carpentry techniques, chairs tended to be straight and upright with tall backs rather than curved, combined with spindles or slats, and occasionally decorated with simple cutout motifs such as spearheads or hearts; the seats were generally covered with simple upholstery, or alternatively leather, rush, or cane.

LEFT In the upper hallway of the same house, the eighteenth-century oak tripod table and child's Windsor chair are below an American folk painting by Sturtevant J. Hamblen, "Boy with a Toy Pull Cart," painted c.1802.

RIGHT The designer Naomi Leff has created a Federal-Revival-style house as a translucent architectural shell to display this wonderful collection of American Queen Anne furniture and naïve paintings. The paintings on the paneled wall are Thomas Skynner's 1846 portraits of Mr. and Mrs. Moses Pike, the chandelier is brass, c.1800, and the carpet is a Beauvais Sultanabad.

LEFT The color of the old paint on the back of a French cupboard is reflected in this collection of nineteenth-century French faience. The plate on the top shelf was made in one of the Quimper factories.

BELOW A nineteenth-century floral shelf edge, which would originally have been used in a shop, decorates a dining-room cabinet. It is filled with raspberry-molded faience plates, creamware, blue-and-white faience, and English enameled glassware.

ARTIFACTS

The style of a grand country house, like its humbler counterpart, rarely indulges in ornament for ornament's sake. Rather it looks to functional objects to provide decoration. In grand country settings, artifacts that were created for a purpose and were at one time useful in day-to-day life—but have long since lost their value as utilitarian objects—may be appreciatively displayed, giving a proud voice to their inherent beauty and to the fine craftsmanship of centuries past. A number of crafts that remain at the forefront of usefulness —quilts, mirrors, ceramic tableware, and lighting fixtures—add pleasure and character

RIGHT: TOP LEFT On a French dining table, this international setting involves a French tablecloth and napkins, an English eighteenth-century amethyst glass carafe, green Italian pressed-glass wineglasses, and English floral-enameled tumblers.

TOP RIGHT With an Elizabethan crewelwork backdrop, this collection of miniature English pieces comprises a painted armoire, a rush-seat spindle chair, Georgian treen (wooden) candlesticks, and an embroidered box.

CENTER LEFT These old French linen napkins have been dyed with traditional woad, now being grown commercially in France and called *bleu de Lectoure*.

CENTER RIGHT A mix of old and new: the nineteenth-century French sofa is covered with a new copy of a Scandinavian fabric; the checked dust ruffle and blue-and-white quilt are new; while the brown-and-white checked quilt is nineteenth-century French.

BOTTOM This table setting has antique glassware and early-nineteenth-century faience plates. It is hard to surpass the subtle colors of these early plates, but many firms now produce reproductions.

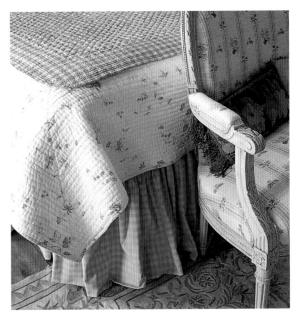

to an interior decorated in rural style. Like everything connected with country style, simplicity and a singular lack of pretension form the cornerstone of this decorative tradition, from a charismatic cottage in Devon to an apartment in the heart of Stockholm to the most elegant farmhouse nestled in the hills of southwestern France.

Among the decorative artifacts that are especially at home in a grand country interior are candlesticks, chandeliers, and fireplace furniture made of brass or silver, marble busts, and tea caddies. The late seventeenth and eighteenth centuries saw a fashion for any number of decorative objects imported from

RIGHT It is often a simple setting with a neutral background that can make you fully appreciate the wonderful quality of early American furniture. The patination and color of this early Queen Anne lowboy is exceptional, as is the early-nineteenth-century Federal convex mirror above with the soaring eagle on high.

OPPOSITE Many times it is the artifacts that bring the theme and style to an interior. In Jerry and Susan Lauren's Manhattan apartment, their fine collection of American weathervanes stands out against the white walls. In this arrangement the vanes appear as sculptures.

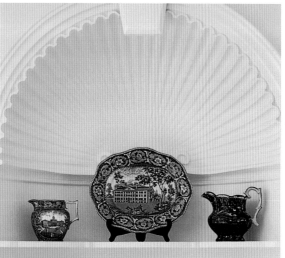

ABOVE AND RIGHT These alcoves (*right*) display a wonderful collection of blue-and-white printed wares made by many of the Staffordshire potteries in England for their American clients. Many of the pieces are from "The Beauties of America" series. The plate above was made by J. and W. Ridgway and depicts the Library, Philadelphia. Other subjects here are New York City Hall and the Deaf and Dumb Asylum, Hartford, Connecticut.

the Far East—lacquerwork furniture, boxes and screens, and blue-and-white Chinese vases and jars that were typically massed on top of cabinets, tables, and wall brackets.

An interior decorated in Arts and Crafts style looks to objects made of leather, pewter, brass, silver, and copper for ornamentation in order to complement the plain, upright furniture. Mirror frames of beaten copper—occasionally ornamented with plain semi-precious stones—or brass candle sconces embellished with designs inspired by medieval motifs recall the handmade articles produced by the designer-craftsmen who worked in the Arts and Crafts guilds. Copper lanterns, pewter candlesticks and jugs, saltglaze pottery, and simple wooden boxes and bowls lend authentic flavor to an Arts and Crafts room. Other typical decorative touches include needlework cushions, and table runnings, window and door curtains, and wall hangings made from yarns colored with natural vegetable dyes. These were usually embellished with motifs inspired by nature, such as birds, animals, and flowers.

Above all else, grand country style celebrates a pride in fine, albeit humble, craftsmanship. The simplicity of a single

LEFT This mid-nineteenth-century tureen, along with its cover and ladle, was transfer-printed in Staffordshire, England, for the very lucrative American market. It depicts the Boston State House.

RIGHT On this typical Directoire stone fireplace sits a nineteenth-century miniature Welsh cabinet and collection of miniature ceramics, alongside a new small lead container.

folk-style painting adorning a wall, a decorative woodcarving, an embroidered box, a snatch of lace, or an embroidered quilt—these reflections of bygone days lie at the heart of country-house decoration. The customs behind folk art have been handed down from generation to generation, and time-honored patterns and designs rarely alter over the years. But this recognition of tradition does not exclude more unusual artifacts, such as Chinese export porcelain, French faience, or Meissen porcelain figurines. This style looks to what is special and what withstands the test of time, to bring color and character to an interior.

ROOMS

Relaxed, informal comfort is the principal ingredient of the country-style room. Nothing should be too precious or studied, for country rooms are, above all else, for living in. They take their cue from the original one-room country dwelling, where the living room was all about living. The conventional day-to-day activities of cooking and eating, sleeping or relaxing, reading, and sharing games and conversation were traditionally conducted in one large room, with all domestic activity revolving around the hearth. This was the nearest most country people came to what is known as a receiving room.

LEFT This dining room in the Dordogne region has a distinctly French feel, with local cedar chairs painted with woad paint. The terracotta tiles are original, as is all the woodwork. Natural soothing colors predominate.

BELOW LEFT The tiled floor and ancient beams are soothed by the creamy yellow on the walls. The furnishings are provincial French and seem made for this room.

Textiles inevitably play a key role in the decoration of a grand country room, following a tradition that flourished from the sixteenth century onward. Sumptuous, richly colored tapestries and hangings add comfort, color, and a sense of luxury to the interior, while the way a variety of fabrics are mixed together—crewelwork, Indian cottons, patchwork quilting, turkeywork, faded silks, velvets, and leather, for example— creates a distinctive country feel. Rooms decorated in the grand country style may also take inspiration from the seventeenth-century French fashion for decorating whole rooms *en suite*—that is, with hangings, tablecovers, and upholstery

ABOVE The designers of the Arts and Crafts movement believed that mechanization had led to a reduction in design quality and construction. Arts and Crafts furniture tended to be made from oak and was often placed in reasonably dark rooms. In this house built in 1898, the walls of the dining room are painted "Amsterdam Green" by Papers and Paints. The room is lifted by the honeyed oak of the hutch and chairs, and the paintings, majolica, and statues.

LEFT In the dining room of this hunting lodge in Périgord, France, the flagstones on the floor were imported from a monastery near La Rochelle. The ceiling has been replaced with linden wood in the traditional way and allowed to age naturally. The walls are color-washed a soft yellow, and all the original woodwork has been painted gray-white. Bright white would be too harsh.

RIGHT While most of this house in Long Island, New York, is painted off-white, the breakfast room has the feeling of a snug. The pine paneling has been waxed to a rich hue, and the country chairs feel welcoming and relaxed.

made in matching fabrics. Floors tend to favor parquet or polished wood, which is then commonly covered with Persian, Turkish, or Savonnerie-style carpets, and walls often feature wallpapers that have been handpainted in the Chinese taste.

On both sides of the Atlantic, the quiet elegance, simplicity, and comfort of the Queen Anne and early Georgian styles are especially at home in a room decorated in the grand country taste. Walls that are paneled frequently incorporate cupboards, while fireplaces and niches might be painted or grained to simulate a more luxurious wood. Symmetry and balance are key features in these gracious, formally arranged rooms: furniture is typically arranged in a symmetrical fashion and set back against the walls. In the eighteenth century, fashionable plasterwork often replaced wood paneling in the most stylish houses, and curtains played a key role in a room's decoration. The most common curtain style was the draw-up, or festoon, curtain, with the

LEFT In the small salon of this French hunting lodge, the walls are color-washed very pale yellow, and the rush matting and linden-wood ceiling are neutral, as is the period stone fire-surround. Color is introduced by plum fabric on the eighteenth-century chairs and screen. The Louis XVI armchair is covered in Le Manch "Messidor."

RIGHT The walls of this large living room are painted ivory, which throws into focus the collection of American Queen Anne armchairs and the amazing molded copper Statue of Liberty weathervane.

FAR LEFT Arts and Crafts style is not always dark and brooding. Here the fire-surround is original to the 1898 house, and the overmantel and Liberty chairs are Arts and Crafts, but the walls are a Farrow and Ball cream, and the sofa bright terracotta. The carpet adds blues.

BELOW In this salon in the Dordogne in France, the eighteenth-century painted screen echoes the colors on the walls, woodwork, and period chairs, whether painted or upholstered.

addition of heavy valances, which would either be covered in fabric that matched the curtains, or carved and gilded. Needlework carpets covered the floors, and embroidered hangings were used for bed curtains. Wallpapers—crimson flocked, imitations of expensive textiles such as tapestry, damask, or Italian silks and velvets, and hand-painted Chinese papers or English imitations printed with chinoiserie designs generally featuring plants, flowers, and birds— were popular fashions for rooms decorated in

the grander country style. This latter taste has endured on into the early years of the twenty-first century.

Commonly found in the light and spacious Arts and Crafts interiors are pale muted colors, traditional wood paneling, natural-colored wooden floors covered with rugs, and rustic stonework. The Arts and Crafts room typically features polished wooden floorboards topped with small handmade needlework rugs featuring designs of stylized flowers and animals or William-Morris–style patterns. Oriental rugs, sisal, and rush matting are equally at home in

ABOVE The natural beauty of the architecture is allowed to be the main feature in this bedroom with its wonderful Périgord chestnut-beam roof structure and floorboards. In these bedrooms in the roof space, the wall color has become even softer, almost cream.

LEFT In high-ceilinged rooms in a French manor house, proportion is improved by a painted dado. The colors are all gently washed to give a softer feel, with the slightly stronger, warmer color below the painted dado rail. In keeping with French tradition, furniture is painted, either allover or, as with the nineteenth-century table on the left, with floral decoration.

this kind of grand country-house interior. Stained-glass panels could make a striking alternative to window curtains. The treatment of walls was closely linked with their structure; features such as the fire-surround, incorporated into the wall treatment, played a decorative as well as a functional role. The whole wall surface might often be painted a uniform pale color, matching the ceiling, and perhaps be embellished with a hand-painted or stenciled frieze.

One of the key characteristics that separates the grander style of country house from its more humble counterparts lies in the luxury of having considerable space for living, with rooms that are especially designated for a variety of pastimes and pursuits: a kitchen, a dining room, a living room, bedrooms, and a bathroom. A palatial apartment in the heart of a city and a spacious farmhouse surrounded by hills and olive trees might revel equally in the more lavish surroundings offered by a generous share of precious space. How this space is decorated, whether it follows urban or rural style or blends the two, is closely connected with the way it responds to daily life and its practical needs.

RIGHT, ABOVE The yellow color-wash on the walls of this house in Périgord is continued into the master bathroom, but here it is given added impact by the blue-and-brown-painted, paneled dado. The nineteenth-century enameled cast-iron rolltop bath would have looked too stark in white and so has been softly washed with blue.

RIGHT In this bathroom the wall colors have again been softly washed, including the rolltop tub with ball-and-claw feet. The wirework shelves are copies of a nineteenth-century original. The Victorian chair has its original faded floral fabric.

Perhaps no other type of interior decoration fulfills the need for a "back to basics" approach to living more than rustic country style. Simple and uncomplicated, self-assured yet without pretension, the style inspired by the rustic rural way of life celebrates the past in a thoroughly modern way. As a living style, it spans the centuries, paying homage to tradition without being frozen in time.

RUSTIC COUNTRY

In essence, rustic country style embraces the rural past. The simple, homespun pleasures of the pastoral life naturally bring comfort and solace, so it is hardly surprising that a home boasting the traditional furnishings associated with country living will evoke a mood of warmth and wellbeing, one that is far removed from the cares and stresses that tend to form an integral part of modern life.

Although it is by its very nature plain and uncluttered, this style does not eschew comfort or the delights of decoration. Rather it looks beyond the dictates of conventional taste and formal period styles, and welcomes what is unique, imperfect, out of the ordinary. It revels in time-worn paint finishes on a cupboard door, a rough-hewn rocking chair, and the scarred oak tabletop that is a reminder of countless family meals taken over many years. Because rustic country style holds a reverence for the rural past and its craftsmanship, what has gone

before is to be celebrated and enjoyed. Beauty and comfort are to be found in simplicity above all else.

The decoration of a rustic country interior can take many different forms, although the main underlying principle remains the same. Objects that ornament a room are practical and functional, rather than pretty but useless trinkets: candlesticks, plates, baskets, and the like. These are the kinds of decorative tools that bring life to the home. Fabrics are simple, and colors plain. The joy is in mixing, adding, and creating an environment that is at once personal and rewards with pleasure.

What probably contributes most to the rustic flavor of a country room is a softness and beauty that has mellowed over the years. An oak table that has acquired a rich, golden patina with time, or the speckled, distressed appearance of old paintwork, lends a spirit of authenticity to the interior.

OPPOSITE: TOP LEFT Worn treads lead up to the bedrooms in this farmer's house from c.1730 in the Hudson River Valley in New York State. The paneling and door are painted with "Salem Brick" from Old Village Paints.

TOP RIGHT Pam Kline had an old Colonial box bed copied for the children's room in her eighteenth-century Dutch house in Columbia County, New York. The linens are by her company, Traditions, and the bed is painted in "Brafferton Blue" from Williamsburg paints.

BOTTOM LEFT This loft apartment in Stockholm, Sweden, is united by white. The chair has a classical Gustavian back and hence hints at Scandinavia, but the overall use of bright white can also give a southern European feel.

BOTTOM RIGHT This seagull decoy is part of an international folk tradition. Made from zinc in the Camargue in France, it is a hunter's confidence decoy: ducks could be persuaded that all was well when they saw these token seagulls apparently undisturbed.

ARCHITECTURE

Simplicity is key to the architecture of the rustic country interior. As with the furniture that goes with this style, the structural elements of the buildings themselves have a feeling of haphazard charm, of taking what is functional and creating something comfortable, decorative, and appealing. Many salient features found in the rooms of a country cottage have been born of necessity: a hearth for warmth and for cooking, for example; a plentiful amount of built-in storage that contributes to the uncluttered feeling essential for living comfortably in a small space; or shutters, placed on the inside of windows, that help keep out the chilly drafts of winter in cooler regions or shade against the excess sunshine of more southerly climates.

A rustic country dwelling makes a virtue of necessity, and celebrates the not-quite-perfect. Key to the general character of a traditional country house that has evolved over time is the need to make use of every inch of space. An interior that has been shaped through the years

ABOVE In Sweden, wood is usually plentiful, and hence massive doors and paneling are common. Woodwork is often painted off-white or a gray-white, with the floorboards left uncovered. The walls are typically hung with canvas, which is then painted to make floral and ribbon panels.

RIGHT In this apartment in Stockholm, Sweden, the architectural details have been brought into the heart of the interior design. Everything is exposed: the beams, the chimney stack, and the brick floor. The previous occupant had tried to conceal them but Martine Colliander decided to use them to visual effect.

by practical requirements, such as the demand for additional living space, will happily absorb any structural changes, additions, or modifications that have been made and use them to decorative effect. A niche beneath the stairs that has been transformed into a cupboard, for example, a chimney corner that has become a pantry, or a staircase that serves a dual purpose by dividing a larger room—such original solutions to fulfilling a need add to the quirky charm of the rustic country dwelling.

The relatively rough and simple character of the walls, ceilings, and floors of a country interior is fundamental to the inherent charm that is country style. Country cottages might typically feature wall paneling painted in light colors or deep earth tones, lime-washed walls of brick or stone, or rough plasterwork along with exposed beams. The distressed look of long-painted woodwork that shows the passage of time, unadorned plank doors and floors, or floors made of brick, stone, or tile—these are all features that highlight the simplicity and pragmatic spirit of the simple rural style.

OPPOSITE PAGE, RIGHT The solid painted fire-surround was put into this Danish house when it was built in 1901. It was situated in the main stairway hall of the house, in order to provide heat upstairs as well.

LEFT AND ABOVE This New-England-style saltbox in Claverack, New York, was built in 1730, with the kitchen and loft added in 1750. The house has post-and-beam and plank-wall construction. The floors could be either wooden boards or brick. The Dutch farmhouse doors are original to the house.

LEFT The Swedish palette has traditionally been known for shades of blues, grays, and off-whites for overall wall cover. These could be plainly washed or on patterned papers. Rose pink, green, and yellow are also found, particularly on floral wreaths and garlands.

RIGHT Bare pink plaster walls can be the perfect backdrops for a rustic country effect. Dark-painted beams, the natural patina of wood, and the colors of old stone slabs all add to this time-worn look.

COLOR AND PATTERN

The color palette adopted for a rustic country interior is extensive and full of variety. Almost any color blends well with country furniture, with earth tones—terracotta and brick, greens, browns, and ochers—especially fitting. The arid climate of hot countries finds fresh relief in white mixed with vivid colors, while in cooler climates pale shades are used to add daylight, or warmth is brought into a room by choosing deep, rich hues.

On the whole, the palette found in the surrounding landscape dictates the colors chosen to decorate a rustic country interior. For example, Swedish Gustavian country style traditionally favors an abundance of various shades of cream, mixed with the pale colors of local flora, such as the pale pink or pale blue of roses and harebells. An American Colonial interior, on the other hand, tends to feature strong, earthy colors—brick reds, terracotta, moss green, deep blue—evoking the natural dyes and pigments used in the eighteenth century. In some regions, paint pigments were traditionally often mixed with, for instance, lime, mellowing the atmosphere.

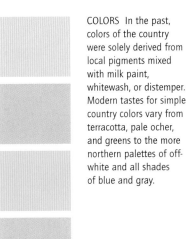

COLORS In the past, colors of the country were solely derived from local pigments mixed with milk paint, whitewash, or distemper. Modern tastes for simple country colors vary from terracotta, pale ocher, and greens to the more northern palettes of off-white and all shades of blue and gray.

Patterns for upholstery fabrics, wallpapers, and decorative blue-and-white tiles take their cue from rural life. In America particularly, flora and fauna were adapted into patterns for textiles or stencil designs. Bold checks, stripes, traditional florals, and provincial prints, along with faded cottons, linens, and ticking, lend that "homespun" feel. A variety of different but complementary patterns in harmonious blends of similar colors, mixed to great effect, lends an air of authenticity and romance. Nothing is too studied or too self-consciously coordinated, and the result is an overall impression of casual charm.

LEFT In the kitchen and dining room of this eighteenth-century Dutch farmhouse, country chairs and table sit on a terracotta tiled floor. The woodwork behind is a very typical soft-green color, which is actually called "Purdy House Gray," by Colonial Williamsburg paints.

RIGHT, ABOVE Against a wash of soft blue and beige sits a wonderful early English chair. It is impossible to ignore the patina of country furniture, which is an addition to the overall color scheme of the room.

RIGHT Swedish country style is about calm and natural colors: whites and off-whites, the terracotta of bricks, and the natural tones of stripped wood.

RIGHT Rustic country style can be created with quite simple furniture: an American nineteenth-century slat-back chair with rush seat; a wooden log basket on aged wooden boards; and paintwork, a specially mixed Colonial red.

BELOW This mid-eighteenth-century English ash-stick chair, with lobster-pot cresting, has the rich color and patination that country enthusiasts adore.

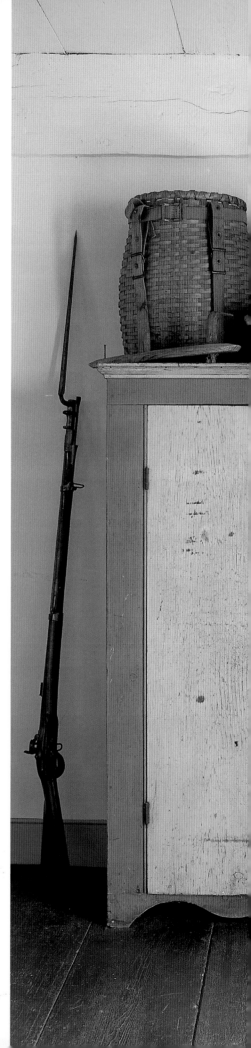

ABOVE RIGHT When a chair has this wonderful patination, color, and honest aging, you can almost feel its history. This chair was made from dug-out elm in the West Country of England in the first half of the eighteenth century.

RIGHT This is a great collection of mainly British country furniture and artifacts from the seventeenth, eighteenth, and nineteenth centuries. From the small oak Welsh grandmother clock to the panel-back dining chair, the decoy ducks, the spice cupboard, the candlestand, and the painted wooden trade sign of a cow with big, soft eyes—all these country pieces tell a story.

RIGHT This simple American painted country desk has a natural craquelure effect. It stands in front of a plank wall, many of its planks salvaged by local shad fishermen from islands in the Hudson River. They were used to separate ice sheets when large volumes of ice were transported down the Hudson to New York.

THIS PICTURE This very simple and yet harmonious nineteenth-century cupboard was painted in ocher and burnt sienna. It is flanked by a slat-back (ladderback) chair.

FURNITURE

In a rustic country interior, furniture need not adhere to any single period. Like the houses themselves, the features that create a room in an authentic country style will usually span the centuries, and rules that dictate whether a piece of furniture is historically accurate do not have a place in this simple, homespun style, unlike in more formal period versions. Country homes were generally furnished over time, with every generation contributing to the overall character of the house. As a result, traditions and memories form the cornerstone of rustic style.

A great deal of the furniture found in traditional country interiors was made by local craftsmen to designs that remained unchanged over the centuries. Much of this furniture would be passed down from one generation to the next, and simple rustic furniture from many different periods and even sources will usually sit happily together.

Although country furniture was first and foremost utilitarian, it did not necessarily lack ornamentation. The solid, practical pieces were often painted, to bring light and color into the interior as well as to mask any deficiencies in the wood. Painted furniture that has developed

LEFT Country living is not all about old furniture—Pam and Tom Kline manage to combine old and new for comfortable living. In the parlor of their eighteenth-century Dutch farmhouse in Columbia County, New York, modern armchairs sit around the old fireplace with bonnet-top chimney. With their slipcovers in blue-and-white ticking, they blend perfectly with the country furniture.

BELOW The Gustavian style in late-eighteenth-century Sweden could be introduced into rural homes as well as great palaces. A particularly fine chair could sit happily with a very utilitarian painted table.

a worn patina over time is particularly at home in a rustic country interior, conveying a sense of the past and adding a bright touch to the room. On some of the most charming examples, layers of paint are partly worn away to divulge a patchwork of faded colors and raw wood.

Typical of the eighteenth-century rustic country interior were the homespun ladderback or slat-back chair, the oak sideboard, the kitchen hutch, the English Windsor chair, and the rocking chair—an American invention. Beds were simple in style, often with a modest form of hangings and covered with quilts. Although some very simple furniture styles are traditionally associated with the countryside, many pieces found in rural interiors were actually provincial adaptations of more fashionable furniture found in the city. These provincial versions often continued to be produced long after the urban style had moved

RIGHT Two pieces from the great tradition of rural crafts: an English comb-back ash and elm Windsor chair, from the Thames Valley, with shaped saddle seat and cabriole leg, probably made around 1760; and a particularly small Welsh grandmother clock, which is both inlaid and painted, and was probably made around 1770.

BELOW Country living allows for inspired reuse. This painted desk has no drawers, but looks quite at home with the painted slat-back (ladderback) chair.

BELOW RIGHT A large cabinet in Stockholm is traditionally painted a cold flat white.

on, and where they might have originally been made in mahogany or walnut, in the countryside the favored lumber was oak, pine, elm, or fruitwoods. In a rustic country home, such furniture would usually have moved farther away from its urban inspiration than that in a grander country dwelling, particularly in the use of local woods and other materials.

Sometimes the eccentricities inherent in the rustic country interior lead to the creation of unusual types of furniture. The Colonial box-frame bed, or built-in closets, for example, would naturally find favor in a country house where space was at a premium.

At the heart of this style lies a celebration of imperfection—nothing should be too studied, too flawless. Woodwork and furniture that have been ripened with age add character and charm to any space.

TOP RIGHT A Welsh spoon rack, c.1800, with original paint contains a collection of cawl spoons. Such displays of every-day objects are characteristic of rustic country style.

RIGHT On a French carved limestone fireplace sit a Welsh pottery pitcher, a hollow-carved decoy of a plover with original paint, c.1860, an English sycamore dairy bowl, c.1760, a gloriously petrified pine platter, c.1700, an English heart-shaped money box, c.1840, an English tavern candlestick with bell, c.1740, and an English solid boxwood taperstick, c.1710.

BELOW An English money box, c.1820, in the form of a bow-fronted Georgian house, sits on an early-eighteenth-century stool-based oak candlestand with a single-plank top. Candlestands traditionally have three legs to enable them to stand on uneven floors. The simple color-wash on the walls complements the wood.

BELOW Objects from different countries and times can be combined if, in essence, they have the same handcrafted tradition. A Welsh ceramic storage jar, c.1840, sits comfortably with an English oak spice chest dated 1696, a collection of matchboxes, a modern bronze bird carving by Guy Taplin, and a large pair of ivorene dice from Florence.

ARTIFACTS

The interior of a country house decorated in a more provincial, rustic style looks to the pastoral tradition for inspiration in decoration as well as for furnishings. The timeless appeal of objects that have been passed down through the generations provides a fitting backdrop for this slice of country life, which honors the earnest work of local craftsmen and artisans. Far from being artless and unsophisticated, the charm of the style lies in its simplicity, a lack of pretension, and a celebration of what was created from necessity.

The inherent beauty of rustic artifacts can be found in the idea that they were made to be functional. A copper pot, a weathervane, a crewelwork quilt—the power of items such as these as decorative objects derives from the fact that they were not originally created to be decorative at all, but to satisfy the basic needs of life. Plates are for eating from, coverlets are for keeping warm, and hand-hammered pots are for cooking in. In the late nineteenth century, William Morris and his colleagues in the Arts and Crafts movement promoted the philosophy that objects made by traditional methods were inherently beautiful, a belief that still resonates today. In the modern world, hectic and unpredictable, a reliance on pieces that brought comfort in times gone by continues to bring comfort to twenty-first-century living on both sides of the Atlantic Ocean.

A feast of country! An itinerant cobbler in western Wales at the end of the eighteenth century would have used this bench as his workshop as he traveled to homesteads and farms. It now houses a pair of French leather shoes and a French shore-bird decoy, both *c.*1860, various early-eighteenth-century treen platters and a fir-cone money box. The nineteenth-century wooden and leather clog again is redolent of rural life.

As a result, many of these artifacts rejoice in showing the inevitable effects of repeated use. Collections of culinary objects—such as gelatin and butter molds, spoons and scoops, or ceramic tableware combined in a variety of vivid patterns —become decorative objects because they reflect the very life for which they were initially created. Battered pewter candlesticks, cooking pots, duck decoys, and weathervanes all evoke the flavor of the country while remaining practical at heart.

All varieties of functional objects found in the rustic country interior play a decorative role. Dried herbs suspended from the wooden beams of a kitchen ceiling, baskets filled with fresh wildflowers, vegetables, or pine cones, storage jars containing spices, and plants in terracotta pots lining a windowsill are what might be called "living" artifacts. Tin chandeliers and copper lanterns provide light, while painted cupboards, blanket chests, boxes, and trunks furnish all-important storage space. Walls hung with picturesque folk paintings, shelves lined with brightly colored local pottery, or faded handmade textiles—hook rugs, quilted coverlets,

A small primitive wrought-iron candlestick is stuck into the paneling, which is painted Old Village "Colonial Green."

and blankets—contribute to the cozy, lived-in atmosphere. Unusual furnishings such as a spinning wheel, a cast-iron stove, and even architectural fixtures—such as hinges, knobs, and latches—can add a decidedly rustic flavor to the spirit of a room decorated in simple country style.

Functional objects used as decoration invite a kind of innocence into the interior. There is no need to impress, to entertain, or to display what is most fashionable. Rather, it is the homespun, rural nature of rustic country style that remains eternally appealing, a comfort and a refuge that is equally at home in a thatched-roofed country cottage or a high-rise apartment in the center of town.

ABOVE There is something particularly delightful about a collection of old decoy ducks, each one hand-carved and painted and with quite distinct personalities. Here Canada geese nest with wigeon, eider, goldeneye, merganser, mallard, and pochard.

LEFT This English hutch from c.1770 has unusual paintwork, with Prussian-blue pigment mixed with casein (a milk-based medium). Architecturally it is also interesting, with pilasters and a glazed front. It contains a collection of Scottish, English, and Irish spongeware.

ROOMS

The real charm of the rustic country cottage lies in those details—soft colors, solid shapes, practical objects—that lend it a relaxed, homey feeling, full of warmth and comfort. It is hospitable, it is unpretentious, and it relies heavily on the traditions of the rural past; the heart of rustic country style can be found in its celebration of the humble craftsmanship of provincial life.

The style that developed in colonial America had much in common with eighteenth-century English country style. The spare, uncluttered rooms of both feature simple rustic furniture, usually made of oak, yew, or fruitwood, plain paneling, clean wall finishes, and a fireplace or open hearth serving as the room's focal point. The naïve simplicity that typifies the rustic country character of the past has a resonance in the twenty-first century, providing a welcome refuge from the stress of modern life and the demands of an ever-changing world.

The timeless appeal of rustic country style finds expression in rooms that are cozy, lived-in, and make virtues out of imperfections. Wall surfaces—which may vary according to local materials and building traditions—uneven, sloping ceilings and floors, and careworn

TOP A farmhouse in northern France houses the collections of antique dealers Laurent Dombrowicz and Frank Delmarcelle. The simple and uncomplicated arrangement of items on the pine butcher's block and the landscapes on the walls create a rural refuge.

ABOVE In a country-style kitchen in Stockholm, everything is neutral and relaxed. From the brick floor and white-painted walls and units to the white and cream glazed faience, the essence is country calm.

RIGHT With a backdrop of ancient oak beams and brick floors, simple French tables and chairs give a refined appeal to this dining area.

OPPOSITE The comforting face of country, with cool colors, a Gustavian sofa, eighteenth-century double doors with distressed paintwork, and a worn brick floor.

LEFT Whites, off-whites, and grays help to create a modern Swedish country style; while considered, this does not in any way feel contrived.

BELOW On this early-eighteenth-century English oak rack and X-frame tavern table, there is a joyous collection of naïve pottery, toys, and treen: children's motto plates, wooden platters, and muffineers.

OPPOSITE Against a color-wash blue background and around an early-nineteenth-century French carved limestone fireplace is Robert Young's collection of eighteenth- and nineteenth-century furniture, pottery, treen, metalware, toys, and books.

woodwork add character to a room. The sense of warmth that defines the interior of a rustic country dwelling has much to do with the use of color: although almost any color, from mellow, pale hues to warm, deep earth shades, can be applied successfully to the walls of a rustic-style room, much depends on the way the paint has been handled—with rough, thick strokes and layers—to produce an authentic country feel.

Brick, flagstone, or tile floors, covered with woven or hooked rugs, painted floorcloths, or rush matting, evoke the enduring appeal of country life, as do the polished or painted wooden floors characteristic of timber-rich regions such as North America and Scandinavia. Adding an important element to the atmosphere is the use of simple rustic furniture. Slat-back chairs (also known as ladderback), paint-scarred tables and cupboards, rough-hewn farm furniture, and the organically inspired designs of the American Adirondacks mix happily together. Useful objects, such as candlesticks, quilts, or old cooking pots, are combined to decorative effect. The sense of permanence and authenticity is underscored by the impression that a room has evolved over time.

MODERN

BY THE 1920s, Frank Lloyd Wright in Chicago, Josef Hoffman in Vienna, and Charles Rennie Mackintosh in Glasgow had pointed to a new direction for architecture and decorative arts: integrated interiors and uncluttered design. This was enthusiastically taken up by artisans of the Bauhaus, founded by Walter Gropius in 1918, which emphasized technology and the need for well-made, practical designs for mass production.

Interiors in the late 1920s and 1930s were also influenced by opulent, streamlined Art Deco. Sumptuous woods such as ebony or walnut were enriched with sharkskin, silver, and ivory, while in the hands of English architect Eileen Gray or Swiss metalworker Jean Dunand, lacquer became a new material paying little heed to the past.

These two divergent paths comprised Modern style. In the 1930s, Bauhaus remained at the heart of Modernism in both Europe and North America, each continent boasting its own style alongside the advantages of technology.

In the 1930s a modified interpretation of Cubism, boasting clean, simple lines and muted color schemes, took hold in interior decoration, as people grew weary of the sumptuous extravagance of Art Deco. A somewhat austere, clinical style —with plain walls, concealed lighting, and geometric forms— came into fashion, largely in reaction to the widespread acceptance of cheap, poorly made versions of Art Deco.

MINIMALISM

The designs of the Bauhaus architects in Germany were initially set apart by their attention to geometric forms; in Bauhaus hands, they generally lacked any ornamentation or, if used, it tended to be uncomplicated and stylized. Perhaps no other designer influenced the fashion for the minimal modern interior more than the Bauhaus architect and designer Ludwig Mies van der Rohe. His "less is more" philosophy found its voice in cubic simplicity of architecture, in a celebration of the natural along with the innovative use of new materials such as glass, plastics, laminated woods, and chromed, stainless, and tubular steel for furniture designs, especially chairs.

Great changes in furniture design occurred during the twentieth century as new manufacturing techniques and materials were introduced. Many of the leading designers— Marcel Breuer, Mies van der Rohe, and Le Corbusier—were also established architects.

Their furniture was tailor-made for modern houses, where space was often at a premium; folding and stacking furniture, for example, was innovative and welcome. Designs were uncluttered, with minimal ornament, and emphasis was on function. The availability of novel, inexpensive materials and modern manufacturing techniques paved the way for forward-looking designs that celebrated the beauty of mass production and rejected the techniques of traditional craftsmen.

Like their Arts and Crafts predecessors, 1920s and 1930s designers championed the integration of a building's furnishings and decoration with its architecture. Yet, unlike the organic vision of the architect Frank Lloyd Wright, whose structures were intentionally designed to blend in with a particular environment, Bauhaus buildings, while harmonious within themselves, frequently seem defiantly at odds with their surroundings.

OPPOSITE: TOP LEFT Poul Kjaerholm's "PK9" tulip chairs were designed in 1961. They show the elegance of structure so typical of Danish furniture designed in the mid-twentieth century.

TOP RIGHT A great example of functionalism and delight, the china in the house of Walter and Ise Gropius makes a modern design statement. As neither of the couple cooked, plastic was chosen, but their real interest was the composition of red, white, gray, and black.

BOTTOM LEFT In Ise and Walter Gropius' daughter's room, simplicity is the key. The bedside table was made in the Bauhaus workshops, and the lamp is American, bought in 1937 from industrial suppliers.

BOTTOM RIGHT Jean Prouve designed the "Antony" chair in 1950. Although now regarded as an icon of mid-twentieth-century design, it was originally intended for commercial use.

MATERIALS

The forward-looking modern architects and designers experimented with conventional materials—wood, natural fibers, and leather—using them in fresh, original ways. They also made imaginative use of industrial materials; the invention of latex foam, for instance, for the motor industry, revolutionized upholstery, as seen in the sophisticated new form of chaise longue that combined latex with preformed bent plywood. This marriage of industry with the domestic widened horizons and pushed the boundaries of creativity.

Materials that readily found a home in the minimalist interior included glass, wood, and concrete, ideal for defining spaces—walls, floors,

LEFT In John Pawson's London house the stairs are tall and narrow, giving an illusion of height. The effect of minimalism is to clear our vision, to allow us to concentrate on texture, form, and color, or lack of it. By its very simplicity, this staircase draws us to the light beyond.

ABOVE This bedroom in the "Trapezoidal House" in New York State leads visually to the silver-birch wood beyond. The eye relishes the lack of clutter and delights in the wooded view. The chaise was purchased in a flea market in New York, and the small table is by Eero Saarinen.

ceilings, and windows—with clean lines. Designers experimented with tubular steel, aluminum, chromium, plastics, and plywood to create streamlined, functional furniture and objects like lamp bases; chairs made use of the blend of strength and lightness in tubular steel and laminated woods, and the result was a radical change in the look of furniture.

Pale woods such as pale oak, maple, birch, and bleached walnut were popular for furniture in the 1920s and 1930s. Expensive pieces were veneered in exotic woods, but decoration was limited mainly to restrained parquetry. Bamboo and sisal floor coverings, woven cane or luxurious leather for sofas and chairs, and granite or marble for tabletops all brought effortless elegance.

FURNITURE

A new economy in furniture design was heralded by the sparseness and purity of the minimalist interior. Marcel Breuer originated the idea for the resilient, springy cantilevered chair made of tubular steel and without back legs, which brought a new transparent dimension to furniture design. Combining comfort and beauty, strength and lightness, it became the prototype for countless versions made with minimal labor, materials, and cost. The seat of this innovative but spare cantilevered chair was most often embellished with luxurious leather, woven cane, or canvas rather than conventional upholstery.

The architect Ludwig Mies van der Rohe was another pioneer in his use of steel for chair designs. He made an elegant version of the cantilevered chair, as well as tables with tubular steel bases. Another of his successful chair designs, which remains in production today, is the elegant "Barcelona" chair (*see page 175*) and stool, constructed with gracefully crossing curved chromium-plated steel bars and leather straps supporting two upholstered rectangular cushions of leather-covered latex foam. Although undeniably modern, its slim, sweeping lines basically adopt the form of

ABOVE The furniture in the Gropius House reflects the cutting edge of 1920s and 1930s design. These bentwood stools were designed by Yanagi in Tokyo in 1925.

RIGHT This collapsible oak-frame chair, with birch-veneered molded plywood seat and back, was designed by Jean Prouve in 1945.

RIGHT, FROM TOP When looking at Poul Kjaerholm's chairs and stools, it is immediately apparent that he first trained as a carpenter. He then studied structure and became fascinated by the possibilities of stainless steel, often cantilevered, with seats of luxurious leather. Although a functionalist, he managed to incorporate humanism into his designs, coupled with Danish sensibilities. The "PK9" chair (*top*) was designed after

Kjaerholm noticed the imprint of his wife's bottom in the sand and realized the perfect shape for the seat of a chair—the ideal blend of form and function. The stacking stool, "PK33," was designed in 1958.

FAR RIGHT Against white-painted eighteenth-century paneling stands an icon of twentieth-century design, also aging rather gracefully. Arne Jacobsen designed this leather chair in the 1950s.

ABOVE In the corner of a bedroom, light plays on the mirrored tile surround of the fireplace. The simple chaise longue is a flea-market find, the table is by Eero Saarinen, and the painting "The Uni-bomber's Shack" by Richard Barns.

RIGHT This could possibly make me a minimalist. The perfect lines of Poul Kjaerholm's "PK24" cane-and-steel chaise longue, designed in 1965, harmonize with the wooden blinds. As with many architects and designers of the twentieth century, Kjaerholm was much influenced by the International style, particularly that of Le Corbusier.

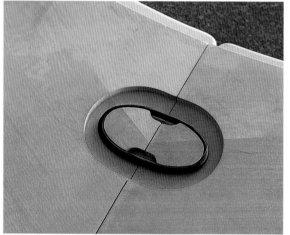

a Roman curule chair or that of a medieval X-frame chair turned sideways. A modern, comfortable classic that fits unobtrusively into a domestic setting, the "Barcelona" applied industrial manufacturing methods to achieve accuracy rather than mass production. It boasts the same precise attention to detail, flawless finish, dignity, and poise found in the buildings created by this very talented architect, which remain hallmarks of modern minimalist style.

One of the most noteworthy advances in chair design during the 1920s was the development of the elegant, form-fitting lounger and reclining chair. The lounge chair by the Finnish architect Alvar Aalto boasted a seat and back formed by a single sheet of

ABOVE The owners, Kathleen Triem and Peter Franck, designed this solid contemporary table for their open-plan living area; the chairs are designed by Karim Rashid. The white walls and flooring with solid wooden window frames lead the eye to the silver-birch woods beyond. The simplicity of the style is reminiscent of Ludwig Mies van der Rohe's principle of "less is more."

laminated plywood bent in sweeping curves and supported on a laminated birch frame. This geometric style was also appropriate for spacious dining tables and other large tables that demanded simplicity of form.

In France, the celebrated architect Le Corbusier produced metal furniture along the lines of Bauhaus designs, but he saw furniture as equipment that should accommodate a variety of uses. His philosophy rested on the premise that a house was a machine designed for living, for convenience and function, and he devised three categories of furniture—chairs, tables, and open or closed shelves—for which he designed a variety of multipurpose forms.

Many Bauhaus furniture designers immigrated to America at the time of World War II. They influenced native designers such as Charles Eames and Eero Saarinen, who, unlike their Bauhaus predecessors, created fluid, friendly shapes that used a minimum of materials and gave a nod to comfort. Even today, the highly original furniture designs of Eames and Saarinen remain at the heart of interiors decorated in a modern, minimalist style. The "LCM" and "DAR" chairs, the "Womb" chair, and the sculptural "Tulip" pedestal chair and table continue to find a home in comfort-seeking interiors, whether in a New York apartment or a French farmhouse.

THIS PAGE Scandinavian designers favored natural materials and furniture with pure lines and a geometric form that could be easily mass-produced. It was a gentler, less intimidating form of modernism. Poul Kjaerholm's main living room in his house in Denmark, designed by his wife Hanne, has effortlessly combined his own furniture in leather, steel, cane, and laminate with natural sisal flooring, white-painted brick walls, and natural wooden beams.

OPPOSITE Neutral colors, natural flooring, and a source of natural light focus the eye on a New York loft's arrangement of mid-twentieth-century classics, such as the "Antony" chair designed by Jean Prouve.

ROOMS

Alongside the luxurious, stylized Art Deco style of the 1920s and 1930s, there emerged the radically different style championed by the avant-garde Swiss-born architect Le Corbusier. His visionary dream of a modern, minimalist architecture found expression in the creation of houses that boasted doors, windows, and other structural features based on a modular system of standard-sized components, containing furnishings that had been mass-produced and walls decorated with abstract paintings.

The character of a room decorated in minimalist style was defined mainly by uncluttered, geometric forms. The recent radical innovations in architecture led to a fundamental transformation of the house interior, with an overall emphasis on function. Furniture and lighting, for example, were integrated with the architecture of a building. Frequently the built-in fixtures could not be distinguished from more adaptable, movable types of furniture. Cabinets, closets, and other types of case furniture might now be supported on plinths or pedestals instead

TOP Walter Gropius was an architect, designer, and the founder of the influential Bauhaus. The main living room in his Massachusetts house is a record of the most influential European design styles between 1920 and 1940. Marcel Breuer made most of the furniture in the room. Gropius believed that architecture and contents were one entity: every bowl, chair, painting, and drape had an essence impacting on the whole.

ABOVE In the Trapezoidal House in New York State, the architects have developed the space to lead uninterrupted through the open-plan interior. Whites, creams, and beige predominate. The high ceilings and light from all sides give an airy and calm aura to this minimal interior. The Astroturf picture on the far wall is by Jane Dickson from New York.

of on legs, and light fixtures were commonly built into walls and ceilings rather than projected or hung. As the use of electric lighting had become widespread, many modern-style designers preferred to fuse light fixtures with the structure of the interior. Made of opaque, smoky glass that was often colored pale blue, pink, or amber to soften and diffuse the brightness, these flush-fitting wall and ceiling lights were generally in geometric shapes and simply appointed, lacking the elaborate pendants and drops favored in the past.

Almost every element—decorative as well as functional—of a minimal modern-style room reflects the philosophy that all should be kept simple, uncluttered, and unadorned. Vases,

ABOVE To be the daughter of Walter Gropius would slightly restrict the choice of decoration, even in your bedroom. Decoration was always restrained and form paramount.

FAR LEFT The overall design concept of this contemporary house is a minimal interior communing with the woods beyond. The vast wall of glass and stainless steel and the expanse of white show influence of European minimalism. Kathleen Triem and Peter Franck designed the Perspex table in the foreground, and the rug below is made from bamboo place mats stitched together.

LEFT The simple structure of white walls and a beige painted floor provides an uncomplicated backdrop for a modern collection of furniture and lighting.

silver services, and ceramic tableware tended to be plain, rounded, or angular geometric forms that were understated and blended easily into the modern interior. Machine-made carpets and rugs also boasted simple geometric patterns in subtle, muted colors that complemented the simplicity of the room rather than producing a dramatic effect.

The architecture of a contemporary interior is most importantly informed by its use. Multifunctional spaces—a living room, dining room, and office combined, for example—are structured with an eye to ever-changing needs. Everything in the room has a purpose; nothing is superfluous. A single wall might be made up of glass panels, bringing light into the room. Slatted wooden screens that can be moved around at will divide up the larger space as necessary. Solid-colored walls provide a spare backdrop for abstract paintings, carpets, and furniture chosen for simplicity and function.

ABOVE In the Gropius House, the bathroom follows the minimalism of the Art Deco period, when the most common backdrop was white, combined with chrome, red, and black.

RIGHT John Pawson believes that architecture should take away unnecessary ornamentation until you are left with the essentials. As William Morris said, "Have nothing in your house that you do not know to be useful and believe to be beautiful."

FAR RIGHT To a minimalist, form and texture create the joy of an interior; superfluous decoration gets in the way of experiencing the space.

ABOVE In an all-white bathroom, Althea Wilson's ceramic wash-hand basin is inspired by a Nigerian *calabash*, which was used to carry milk.

RIGHT In this bathroom designed by Hanne Kjaerholm in 1959, the muted gray marble tiles impose a unity and, while ultimately practical, retain a sense of warmth.

Although many features distinguish the minimalist interior, materials separate it from its traditional counterparts. The innovative architects and designers who brought life to modern dwellings pushed the boundaries of design, both with new materials such as steel and with new ways of using conventional fabrics and materials. These champions of the new and unusual are set apart by their imaginative approach, taking something intended for one function and opening up new possibilities by using it in a wholly new way. Their holistic philosophy created a unified design from a diversity of materials, modern and traditional, and synthetic as well as natural.

The confluence of different textures—woven floor mats, painted brick walls, marble-topped tables, wooden window blinds, leather-covered cushions—brings warmth to the minimalist interior. It is its serenity and simplicity that give comfort and lend credence to Ludwig Mies van der Rohe's philosophy that "less is more."

When modernist philosophy met classicism, a distinctive style came into being. Modernism need not mean minimalism, nor does it demand rejection of history. The art and architecture of ancient Greece and Rome in particular are at home with the strong lines of a modern interior. At the heart of the blend is an aesthetic compatibility that offers creative expression and harmonious composition.

CLASSICAL MODERNISM

The neoclassical architecture and furnishings—echoes of classical antiquity—fashionable from the last years of the eighteeenth century may seem strikingly familiar to modern eyes. The styles of the French Directoire, Early Empire, American Federal, and English Regency periods, for example, boast a very contemporary feel: pared down to bare essentials and sparsely ornamented, these clean-lined, rather sober brands of neoclassical style resonate with modern sensibilities, and marry perfectly with up-to-the-minute interiors and modern paintings and sculptures. Later neoclassical style, too, is at home with a range of modern furnishings and objects from broad vocabularies of decorative art and ornament.

A contemporary interior that looks to classical antiquity for inspiration revels in the harmony and principles of proportion that lie at the heart of the architecture of ancient Greece and Rome. But at the root of the doctrine of modernism has always been the desire to render the home as "a machine for living in," a philosophy famously championed by the forward-thinking architect Le Corbusier. The marriage of these two very different philosophies results in a unique and highly imaginative concept for the design and decoration of an interior.

Contemporary decoration of rooms in a way that pays homage to the classical past—along with complementary furnishings and decorative objects that bring them to life—takes a fresh and original look at what came before while celebrating the novel and the new. Living in the present, encouraged by the freedom and individuality celebrated in today's world—using unusual materials, appropriating decorative elements from the antique vocabulary, and mixing them at will—classical modernism also pays tribute to the essential qualities of the classical past: harmony, clarity, and imagination.

OPPOSITE: TOP LEFT Glimpses of a deliberate classical style: the marble fireplace is 1820s, with a bronze medallion, a French Empire candlestick, and a stone finial. It is the juxtaposition that gives a strongly twentieth-century feel.

TOP RIGHT A pickled oak table and stools made in France in the 1940s. The bulbous legs with scrolling capitals are typical of the period.

BOTTOM LEFT This is an elongated gazelle's-head terminal on a 1940s stool in wrought iron. It is an iconic emblem of mid-twentieth-century classicism.

BOTTOM RIGHT Again, the combination of items is testament to the style: the Gabriella Crespi vase made in Milan in the 1960s, the urn-shaped lamp, the Lalique black panther, and the nautilus shell.

RIGHT A wrought-iron chair with off-white canvas upholstery sits on a brightly colored Aubusson carpet designed by André Arbus in the 1940s.

BELOW In the home of the creators of B&B Italia, this grand staircase exudes quality and simplicity. Just as in the past, there is a glory in the figuration of wood, and the simple banisters merely emphasize the quality of the materials; there is no need for decoration.

MATERIALS

The modern classical interior depends on a wide variety of fabrics, juxtaposing traditional materials of antiquity, such as marble and bronze, with the more exotic and unpredictable —such as Oriental lacquer, shagreen, wrought iron, and leopard skins. Mixing the conventional with the contemporary makes a bold statement and means that the styles will not be mistaken for anything other than thoroughly modern. Classical modernism owes much to the mood of Art Deco, and often uses colors that echo Art Deco as well as the strong colors used by the ancients, as it brings together diverse and disparate materials in fresh combinations.

It is the imaginative and visionary ways that very different materials—organic and industrial, for example—are used or combined that brings life to a classically inspired modern room. A chair of wrought iron embellished with the head of a sphinx pays homage to the past and yet remains unquestionably contemporary. What delights the most is the freedom of looking at an authentic classical form and revitalizing it by using materials that have nothing to do with classicism. Employing unusual fabrics and materials with an eye to transforming a traditional design into something unequivocally up-to-date and modern is exactly that: modern. The contemporary interior does not shy away from the trend of taking inspiration from the unconventional. Rather, it celebrates the unusual—hard-wearing canvas is used as upholstery fabric, for example, while a bold modern sculpture is rendered in glass, and a lamp base is constructed in gilt metal in the shape of a tree. In each case, new materials are used on traditional forms with confidence, panache, and a sense of style.

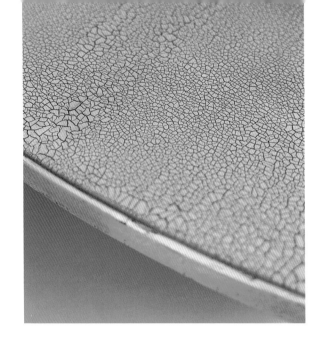

LEFT The scheme for this bathroom comes from the red and gray marble that Yves Gastou found in the Languedoc region of France. The pale gray above and the colors of the bathtub are all taken from the striations in the marble.

TOP AND ABOVE This shagreen-covered table (*above*) was designed by Sonja Caproni, inspired by Art Deco examples. The dressing-table set is silver-mounted old shagreen. A similar surface is created on another table (*top*), which is silvered glass with a craquelure effect.

FURNITURE

Furniture in a classically modern interior takes inspiration from forms that echo the antique past, but are rarely direct imitations of it. Rather, it draws quotations from classical vocabulary—a dramatic pediment on an architectural bookcase, for example, a console table on fluted columns, a stool made from wrought iron and decorated with swans' heads, or a chair of blackened wood boasting armrests embellished with an Egyptian sphinx—and creates something modern and new. One would hardly call a seventeenth-century refectory-style table with legs in the form of antique urns topped by architectural Ionic capitals "classical," because no such furniture existed in the ancient world —or indeed, in the neoclassical fashions of the late eighteenth and early nineteenth centuries —yet the references are unmistakable. And it is this kind of celebration of the architecture and decorative motifs of antiquity that finds a comfortable home in a modern interior.

Contemporary furniture shaped by classicism shares with its antique ancestors the fundamental virtues of harmony, purity of line,

FAR LEFT This leather-covered desk is new but inspired by the Art Deco style, and the objects on it conform to the style. The small French X-frame stool is covered in tiger-print fabric.

LEFT This marble column and 1940s French chair in a house in southwestern France designed by Yves Gastou show the refined quality of the works created in this period.

BELOW LEFT A console table with fluted columns, made from multicolored marble from the Languedoc region of France, with a wooden shaving mirror, stone urn, and brass candlesticks. These cameos are classically inspired and in keeping with a room of the mid-twentieth century.

BOTTOM LEFT A realistically carved oak cabinet by Jacques Adnet stands on leafy cast-bronze legs. This superb example of 1940s design is surmounted by marble tazzas.

RIGHT A 1940s ebonized Egyptianesque fauteuil armchair by André Arbus dominates a corner of a drawing room designed by Yves Gastou. The neutral colors of the walls, plain wooden flooring, and subtle drapes allow the elements of classical decoration, such as the urns, obelisks, marble-topped table, and wonderful black-and-gilt mirror to make full impact.

ABOVE An American 1950s chair found in a flea market has been given a good polish and upholstered in a fashionable leopard print. The zebra rug fits with the theme. The table has an ivorene shagreen finish, all adding to this reserved 1930s classical feel.

LEFT This room relishes the neoclassical. It is a statement of the beauty and proportion of classical ornament: the damaged angel, the eighteenth-century flaming urn on a marble column, the marble bowl, and, dominating it all, the wonderful pickled-oak table and stools by the great 1940s designer Jean-Charles Moreau.

minimalism, something which is decidedly absent in the grander, full-blown versions of classicism that emerged in the past.

This modern vision of classicism is expressed in details. An X-frame stool based on the Roman curule form is upholstered with tiger-skin fabric—inspired by the antique, but wholly French in concept. A table is supported on a single pedestal in the form of what appears to be a classical column—but is not. A modern oak cabinet is embellished with a carved narrative that vaguely recalls the marble relief sculptures of ancient Greece. A robust plinth with straight lines in variegated marble appears identical to an architectural column that helped support the portico of a Roman temple—but not quite. Pickled oak stools reminiscent of the classical X-frame form actually boast the cabriole legs and serpentine apron of French Rococo. A comfortable-looking, well-proportioned chair that conjures an image of the Roman curule chair with curved legs and a fluid frame looks suspiciously like the deck chair that today is at home on a beach or ocean liner. Contemporary furniture made for the classically modern interior enjoys the very best from two worlds.

and simplicity. At first glance it may seem to be a replica of any one of a number of historical styles—Italian Renaissance, Baroque, or various strands of neoclassical—that drew inspiration from ancient Greece and Rome. However, on closer inspection it becomes apparent that this classical taste is really very modern in spirit. At its heart lies the fundamental doctrine of

BELOW LEFT For the modern classical interior, light is essential. In this library designed by B&B Italia, further interest is added with the contrasting black/brown and white of the woodwork and zebra rugs.

BELOW In the corner of the master bedroom of this house in southwestern France, contemporary vases in porcelain and alabaster sit on a neoclassical pickled-oak cabinet by Jean-Charles Moreaux, designed in the 1930s. The wrought-iron chair was designed by André Dubreuil.

ROOMS

Interiors decorated with an eye to antiquity rely on a variety of interpretations of the classical past, while remaining ever mindful of their place in the modern world. Always with a twist, a unique spin that sets them apart from their eighteenth-century neoclassical counterparts, these rooms demonstrate the classical clarity of line that furnishes an uncluttered, complementary background for an eclectic mixture of furniture, artifacts, and art.

The contemporary feel of the style can be found in the attention paid to ceilings, walls, and floors, which help to establish the classical setting. Treatments such as painted wall panelings, as well as floors made of

ABOVE LEFT This room shows the immense power of the neoclassical furniture and textiles made by André Arbus in the 1940s. The grand cabinet has many classical features but a distinctly modern feel. The black lacquer table with gold detailing on the border sits on a strongly colored Aubusson carpet with geometric design, again by André Arbus. Throughout the room there are many classical references.

LEFT It is the confident mix of furniture from different periods and styles that gives a sense of visual delight.

ABOVE This living room in a house designed by B&B Italia is a feast of contrasting textures and media. The rugs soften the hard lines of the floor. Curves compete with straight lines. Mesh screens filter light while giving privacy, and are echoed in the doors of the bookcases. The red upholstery complements the wood paneling and helps to add warmth, providing a foil to the chrome, white, and black.

RIGHT This library bookcase was designed by André Arbus in the 1940s with a characteristic dramatic broken pediment. The room is home to many collections as well as books and seems to echo the Grand Tours of the eighteenth and nineteenth centuries.

geometrically patterned oak parquet, stone, marble, or lime-washed wood, combine the clean, streamlined ambience of modern design with traditional materials.

A classically modern look can also be achieved by combining stylistic elements that originated during the later, more opulent neoclassical period with a modern architectural framework and twentieth-century furniture designs. Although stylistically diverse, these share the clean lines and symmetry of classical architecture that is central both to neoclassical taste and to the philosophy of the minimalists.

A room that embraces the modern alongside the classical celebrates the qualities they share: clean lines, symmetry, harmony, and balance.

The geometric shapes and mathematical proportions that define the art and architecture of classical antiquity are equally at home in a twenty-first-century interior. These ancient principles are expressed in a variety of ways that highlight the marriage of the classical and the modern. Volumes of books, for instance—in square and rectangular shapes—line a wall. The colorful geometrical pattern of a carpet adorns the floor. Furnishings are arranged symmetrically within an architecturally informed space: square tables, rectangular-shaped windows. Such a room is also furnished with modern interpretations of classical furniture designs—a delicate side table, for example, although made from the relatively

modern material of wrought iron, boasts the cabriole legs which look back to mid-eighteenth-century furniture designs. An *escritoire* recalls the robust, bold dimensions of an ancient Greek temple, although its broken pediment, squat proportions, and Gothic arches point to an amalgam of several styles deriving from different periods.

Looking back to antiquity while embracing the future—this imaginative style of interior decoration at heart celebrates the minimal, the modern, and the pure. At the same time, it delights in the beauty, charm, and integrity that informed the art and architecture of the classical past. Past and present find shared principles, and the result is a harmonious whole.

ABOVE This bedroom has a distinctly 1950s glamour look. With tones of gray and off-white, it is cool and understated. The white-painted chairs, with a hint of English Regency, are actually 1940s American; the table base is a reconstituted stone tassel.

RIGHT A tub to wallow in. This copper bathtub, which was made at the beginning of the twentieth century, is backed by grey French marble. Neoclassical busts, figures, and motifs surround it.

By the early 1960s, discreet, practical "good taste" and the standards associated with high quality were beginning to be supplanted by a fashion for witty, disposable, and inexpensive designs for furniture and objects. Bold, abstract patterns and vivid psychedelic colors were brought together in a variety of unusual and often jarring combinations, resulting in a blithe, lighthearted approach to decoration.

THE 1960s AND 1970s

At the heart of this new, unconventional notion of what constitutes "style" lay a sense of humor and a high-spirited vision of freedom from orthodox standards that traditionally defined good taste, along with a knack for turning the constraints of polish, refinement, and sophistication upside down. Not only were the boundaries of what was generally acknowledged to be acceptable good taste pushed to their limits in the revolutionary decades of the 1960s and 1970s, but everything—from the shapes of furnishings and decorative objects to the materials that they were made of—challenged the prevailing ideas of what constituted a warm, comfortable interior, or even what it was possible to make into an interior. The designers and decorators who charted unexplored territory in the realm of interior design were often richly rewarded with recognition for their inventiveness, their bravado, and their willingness to stimulate and provoke.

The influence of kitsch and pop art of this period led to the creation of a string of preposterous, eccentric designs whose appearance gave no clue to their function. But, rejecting the basic philosophy of form following function that lay at the heart of the Bauhaus designs in the early twentieth century, these forward-thinking, imaginative architects of a new kind of decoration were not concerned with what was practical. Instead they brought an original and modern slant to the conventional, which was perceived as ordinary and run-of-the-mill. This they accomplished by using modern materials— plastics, laminated woods, and plywoods, for example—for their unusual designs.

These pioneering designs for furniture and interior decoration that emerged in the 1960s and 1970s remain influential catalysts for redefining style and nudging the frontiers of what is modern into the twenty-first century.

OPPOSITE: TOP LEFT Ludwig Mies van der Rohe's "Barcelona" chairs were designed in 1929 for the German Pavilion at the International Exhibition in Barcelona. Regarded as modern classics, they were reissued by Knoll in 1948. John Barman commissioned these in cherry red. In the background is an op-art-inspired silvered acrylic bubble screen.

TOP RIGHT These yellow 1970s chairs were also made in orange. The light was inspired by Verner Panton's "Moon" Lamp.

BOTTOM LEFT The orange bed is an example of how designers of the 1960s relished departing from the purity and white of the minimalist modernists. This was the era of being at the forefront of fashion, of being "cool."

BOTTOM RIGHT Mies van der Rohe designed these chairs for Fritz and Grete Tugendhat's home in Brno, Czechoslovakia, between 1929 and 1930. The steel had to be very heavy gauge in order to support the cantilevered structure. They were reissued by Knoll in 1960.

ABOVE This house is organic; one pod leads to another. At the center is the stairwell covered in Vallauris stoneware tiles. This is all about contrasting textures and shapes. The undulating hall ceiling is draped in red jersey. The stair walls are covered with beige carpet and lit by a concealed lighting strip behind the banister.

LEFT In the 1950s and 1960s, form, texture, and color were vital ingredients for the well-designed interior. Here John Barman has contrasted the tones and geometric shapes of the rug with the steel and white cut-pile fabric of the chair.

LEFT, BELOW An op-art screen formed with silvered acrylic bubbles causes interesting reflections and distortions.

MATERIALS

The innovative decades of the 1960s and 1970s witnessed designers applying a wide variety of newly invented materials to cover walls, upholster chairs, make a table, and furnish a bed. These materials were quite frequently combined with a medley of age-old, hard-wearing fabrics that were brought new life by use in decidedly unconventional ways.

Cost-effective plastics, acrylics, chrome, Plexiglass, aluminum, metal wire, and mirror glass—these are but a few examples of modern materials that were adopted to create unusual versions of everything from walls and floors to seats and cabinets. Any kind of material was fair game, whether employed in a piece of furniture, a table top, a chair, a light fixture, or the structure of a ceiling. Wood was treated like plastic; upholstery was made of vinyl or fabric-covered latex foam; while paper and fiberglass were appropriated for walls, beds, and screens.

Alongside man-made materials were natural and organic ones—pale-colored stones or small chunks of wood designed to create the impression of parquet flooring. The traditional practice of contrasting textures for decorative effect was now taken up, with the intention of marking out a single, unusual texture as an essential focus of decorative interest.

LEFT The swimming pool is original to this 1970s house. There are mirrored panels on the walls and a Plexiglass ceiling. Different-colored concealed lights play visual games with the mirrors and water. The massive aluminum opening doors lead to the garden and lake.

RIGHT Now used as a window blind in the Normandy house, this "para vent" screen of twisted Plexiglass was originally a room-divider in the BNP bank in Paris in the 1970s.

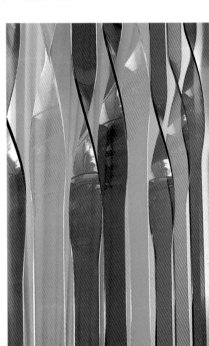

FURNITURE

Like almost everything that characterized the decades of the 1960s and 1970s, the design of furniture underwent a revolution. As with architecture, the strictly functional approach defined by the Bauhaus designers gave way to new principles defining beauty, taste, and art. For furniture, this meant a shift away from rigid geometric forms toward highly individual, sculptural shapes; bold use was made of bright colors, taking inspiration from pop art and the taste for kitsch. No material was immune from the imaginative experiments of these forward-looking, adventurous furniture designers.

Experiments with bright colors and unorthodox shapes led to the creation of many exciting and witty furniture designs, especially

LEFT Again a furniture classic, the "Egg" chair and ottoman were originally designed by Arne Jacobsen between 1957 and 1958 for the Royal SAS Hotel in Copenhagen. The chair makes a strong sculptural statement. It is formed from molded fiberglass polyurethane, upholstered with latex foam, and was originally covered with leather. It can tilt and swivel on its cast-aluminum base. This chair and ottoman have been produced by Fritz Hansen since 1958.

BELOW In the main living space of this apartment in New York, the sharp 1960s palette of black, red, charcoal, and white is set off against a white background. The modern rug by Angela Adams has a very 1960s feel.

ABOVE This pristine dining room skillfully mixes 1960s, 1970s, and new pieces. The brushed-aluminum table is new, while the Lucite dining chairs, based on a 1934 design, Italian wall sconces, and credenza designed by Tommi Parzinger are all 1970s. The glass is mid-twentieth-century Murano.

RIGHT With white walls, resin floor, two-tone gray rug, Italian table, and "Tulip" chairs designed by Eero Saarinen between 1955 and 1956, this dining area is calm and unfussy. The chairs, with their plastic-coated cast-aluminum base supporting a molded fiberglass seat shell, allowed Saarinen to clean up the "slum of legs."

in the domain of seat furniture. The plastic "Swan" and "Egg" chairs designed by Arne Jacobson in the late 1950s gave way to the bright spirit of the 1960s, which was effectively captured in the Italian "Blow" chair created by Donato d'Urbino, Paolo Lomazzi, and Jonathan de Pas. A transparent, inflatable chair made of PVC and covered in leather, it challenged the entire concept of seating as solid and permanent. A similar type of chair created by Peter Murdoch in Britain was the "child's chair": made from one flat piece of laminated paperboard and decorated with a contemporary op-art polka-dot pattern, it could be mass-

BELOW This bedroom in a New York apartment is a blissful antithesis of the bright styles of the 1960s and 1970s. The reflective black and gray tones contrast with the white. Here the emphasis is on womblike slumber. From some angles, the mirrors behind the headboard provide glimpses of the constantly changing Manhattan skyline.

ABOVE In the master bedroom of this 1970s house in France, Emmanuel Renoird has captured the essence of the period. The round bed is French, the small tables were designed by Saarinen for Knoll, and the orange screen hiding a radiator is very 1970s. The glimpse of Andy Warhol's picture of Marilyn Monroe sets the scene of the 1960s. The chair is orange Plexiglass, made in Italy in the 1960s.

produced quickly and cheaply, and was disposable —all qualities that were championed by the new popular culture. Other unusual designs for chairs included the "Sacco," a kind of sack resembling a beanbag made from leather or plastic that was loosely filled with granules of styrofoam; the unusual "Dondolo" rocking chair, molded in fiberglass; and the plastic single-piece cantilevered chair designed by Eugene Panton.

Influenced by pop art and kitsch, some wacky and unpredictable furniture designs gave no hint as to their function. Among these were the "Joe" sofa—designed in the shape of a huge baseball glove—and the brightly painted candy-striped rectangular armoires and cupboards made of plywood and laminated plastic by Ettore Sottsass, as well as Sottsass' plastic "Cometa" sculptured floor lamp.

Popular in the 1960s were the futuristic seating systems designed by Joe Colombo. These were made of foam cushions covered in stretch fabrics that could be grouped in any number of ways to create a flexible and informal arrangement of furniture that was especially appropriate for smaller living spaces.

The traditional bedstead became obsolete during this period, as a simple rectangular or—more imaginatively—round mattress with no headboard and a brightly colored coverlet came into fashion, testifying to the very modern preference for convenience and simplicity without sacrificing comfort. Plain, geometric-shaped nightstands supported lighting novelties, of which the "lava lamp" is perhaps an extreme example, although it effectively symbolizes the psychedelic atmosphere of the 1960s and 1970s.

The joy of 1970s style is well expressed in this stylish bedroom. The painting is by Geneviève Glaisse, the molded polyester bed was designed by Marc Held for Prisunic edition 1970, and the bedspread was designed by Emmanuel and called "Le Lapin Rouge."

What is surprising about this interior, with its polished resin floor, modern scarlet "Alfa" sofas by Zanotta, yellow 1970s chairs, and "Arctic Peaks" ceiling with concealed multicolored lights, is that it was designed between 1973 and 1976 in rural Normandy, in northern France. The house was built for a rich contractor's son who had spent some time in San Francisco. It has been restored by Emmanuel Renoird to reflect what was good about the 1970s—the shapes, colors, and textures, not the clutter.

ROOMS

The revolutionary 1960s and 1970s brought about a whole new way of looking at space and the relationship between architecture and design. Confident rethinking of interiors went far beyond the demolishing of walls and knocking through rooms and then filling them with experimental, avant-garde furniture. A fundamental tenet of the time was to structure an interior so as to maximize the space and accommodate a busy, multilayered lifestyle.

The primary intention behind the "open-plan" interior that gained favor in the 1960s and 1970s was to create a feeling of spaciousness. But one of the main challenges when confronted with a vast expanse of space was how to create separate areas for a range of

ABOVE Frédéric Méchiche has designed an interesting environment in his apartment in the Marais district of Paris. By buying authentic period features, he first created a late-eighteenth-century Directoire duplex in a rather soulless 1960s building. The salvaged neoclassical fire-surround, with overmantel of pilasters, carved fan design, and bare floorboards, provide an interesting backdrop for modern classic furniture including Ludwig Mies van der Rohe's "Barcelona" chairs.

activities: living room, dining room, kitchen, and office. Without walls, the open plan needed to find other ways to organize and define space.

One imaginative and highly successful method was to use movable screens or panels to designate specific areas for work or leisure activities. Constructed in a variety of new materials—plastics, Plexiglass, mirror glass, and acrylic, for example—screens could be moved about to arrange interior spaces at will, and rearrange them as needed, while also serving as an unusual decorative backdrop.

Another obvious but effective means was through furniture. Grouped and placed for maximum impact, furniture could set the boundaries for each separate area, creating a sense of seamlessly moving from room to room without the fixed demarcation of walls.

Color and light also played a role in defining space. In an interior painted brilliant white, for example, a limited palette of bright colors for furnishings—such as black, red, and charcoal gray—strengthened the structure of each individual space, while colorful abstract art and ornaments broke up wide, flat surfaces. Light divided a large area into smaller, inhabitable sections by illuminating spaces with concealed strips, domed reflectors, or acrylic globes.

The interior of the 1960s and 1970s indulges in a sense of humor and surprise. Walls, floors, and ceilings rely on unusual materials: for example, floors are made of polished concrete or resin; walls might be covered with acrylic carpet fabric; and ceilings are not flat but draped in brightly colored jersey or constructed in three-dimensional wood or plastic in unusual configurations. Fresh and modern, colorful, clean and uncluttered, functional and stylish—interiors of the 1960s and 1970s were all about shapes, textures, colors, and patterns.

ABOVE In the hallway of this 1970s house in Normandy, the white walls reflect the red-jersey undulating ceiling as it leads to the woods beyond. The seating is from an airport waiting room, and the chrome light was bought in the south of France.

LEFT This bathroom in a master bedroom has original orange and black decoration. The shower area has small red/orange tiles. The ceiling was constructed from bits of wooden parquet placed at odd angles.

OPPOSITE This womblike bedroom looks over the skyscrapers of Manhattan. The black walls have a comforting sheen, and contrast with the yellow Ludwig Mies van der Rohe chairs with red and white shag-pile pillows.

DIRECTORY

MUSEUMS USA

Bartow Pell Mansion
Shore Road, Pelham Bay Park,
Bronx, NY 10464
Tel: +1 718 885 1461

The Belvedere Mansion
1008 Park Ave, Galena, IL 61036

The Brooklyn Museum of Art
200 Eastern Parkway, Brooklyn,
NY 11238-6052
Tel: +1 718 638 5000
www.brooklynmuseum.org
28 period rooms from a 17th-century
Brooklyn Dutch farmhouse to a 20th-
century Art Deco library designed by
Alavoine of Paris and New York.

Drayton Hall
3380 Ashley River Road,
Charleston, SC 29414
Tel: +1 843 769 2600
www.draytonhall.org

Historic Deerfield
Deerfield, MA 01342
Tel: +1 413 774 5581
www.historic-deerfield.org
There are 14 museum houses showing
many aspects of early New England life.

Melrose
Natchez National Historical Park,
Melrose Avenue, Natchez, MS 39121
Tel: +1 601 442 7047

**The Metropolitan Museum of Art,
New York**
1000 Fifth Avenue at 82nd Street,
New York, NY 10028
Tel: +1 212 535 7710
www.metmuseum.org

Nathaniel Russell House
51 Meeting Street, Charleston,
SC 29401
Tel: +1 843 723 1623

**The Winterthur Museum,
Garden and Library**
Route 52, Winterthur, DE 19735
Tel: +1 800 448 3883
www.winterthur.org

MUSEUMS UK

The American Museum
Claverton Manor, Bath, Avon
BA2 7BD
Tel: +44 (0)1225 460503
www.americanmuseum.org
The museum is a series of diverse and
authentically furnished rooms tracing
the American way of life from Colonial
times to the mid-19th century.

The Geffrye Museum
Kingsland Road, London E2 8EA
Tel: +44 (0)20 7739 9893
www.geffrye-museum.org.uk
The museum houses permanent displays
of period rooms in England from 1600
to the present day.

Leighton House
12 Holland Park Road,
London W14 8LZ
Tel: + 44(0)20 7602 3316
Leighton_House_Museum@rbkc.gov.uk
The former studio-house of the
Victorian artist Frederic, Lord Leighton
(1830–96), its sumptuous interiors are
hung with paintings by Leighton,
Millais, and Burne-Jones. Don't miss
my favorite—the Arab Hall.

Osterley Park
Jersey Road, Isleworth,
Middlesex TW7 4RB
www.nationaltrust.org.uk
Designed by the architect Robert Adam
in 1761, today it displays some of the
most complete examples of Adam
interiors.

Sir John Soane's Museum
13 Lincoln's Inn Fields,
London WC2A 3BP
www.soane.org
Built by the architect as his home, it still
houses his antiquities and works of art.

Victoria and Albert Museum
Cromwell Road, South Kensington,
London SW7 2RL
Tel: +44 (0)20 7942 2000
www.vam.ac.uk
One of the world's great museums
of the applied and decorative arts.

The Wallace Collection
Hertford House, Manchester Square,
London W1U 3BN
Tel: +44 (0)20 7563 9500
www.the-wallace-collection.org.uk
Houses a wonderful collection of art
assembled by one family, including
French 18th-century furniture,
paintings, porcelain, and works of art.

**Weald and Downland
Open Air Museum**
Singleton, Chichester, West Sussex
PO18 0EU
www.wealddown.co.uk
Tel: +44 (0)1243 811363
The museum has 45 historic buildings
dating from the 13th to the 19th
centuries, many with period gardens.

US AUCTIONEERS

CALIFORNIA
Bonhams & Butterfields
7601 Sunset Blvd, Los Angeles,
CA 90046-2714
Tel: +1 323 850 7500
www.butterfields.com

Bonhams & Butterfields
220 San Bruno Ave, San Francisco,
CA 94103-5018
Tel: +1 415 861 7500
www.butterfields.com

eBay, Inc.
2005 Hamilton Ave, Ste 350,
San Jose, CA 95125
Tel: +1 408 369 4839 staff@ebay.com
www.ebay.com

IDAHO
The Coeur d'Alene Art Auction
PO Box 310, Hayden, ID 83835
Tel: +1 208 772 9009
www.cdaartauction.com

MAINE
James D. Julia Auctioneers Inc.
Rte 201, Skowhegan Rd, PO Box 830,
Fairfield, ME 04937
Tel: +1 207 453 7125
www.juliaauctions.com

MASSACHUSETTS
Fontaine's Auction Gallery
Pittsfield, MA
Tel: +1 413 448 8922
www.craftsman-auctions.com

Skinner, Inc.
357 Main St, Bolton, MA 01740-1104
Tel: +1 978 779 6241
www.skinnerinc.com

Willis Henry Auctions, Inc.
22 Main St, Marshfield, MA 02050
Tel: +1 781 834 7774/800 244 8466
www.willishenry.com

MISSOURI
Ivey-Selkirk
7447 Forsyth Blvd, Saint Louis,
MO 63105
Tel: +1 314 726 5515
www.iveyselkirk.com

New Hampshire
Northeast Auction
694 Lafayette Rd, P O Box 363,
Hampton, NH 03483
Tel: +1 603 926 9800
www.northeastauctions.com

New Jersey
Craftsman Auctions
333 North Main Street,
Lambertville, NJ 08530
Tel: +1 609 397 9374
www.ragoarts.com

Rago Modern Auctions,
LLP 333 North Main Street,
Lambertville, 08530
Tel: +1 609 397 9374
www.ragoarts.com

NEW YORK
Christie's
502 Park Ave, New York, NY 10022
Tel: +1 212 546 1000
www.christies.com

William Doyle Galleries
175 East 87th St, New York,
NY 10128-2205
Tel: +1 212 427 2730
www.doylegalleries.com

Framefinders
454 East 84th Street, New York,
NY 10028
Tel: +1 212 396 3896
www.framefinders.com

Sotheby's
1334 York Ave, New York,
NY 10021
Tel: 212 606 7000
www.sothebys.com

Swann Galleries, Inc.
104 East 25th St, New York,
NY 10010-2977
Tel: +1 212 254 4710
www.swanngalleries.com

PENNSYLVANIA
Alderfer Auction Company
501 Fairground Rd, P O Box 640,
Hatfield, PA 19440-0640
Tel: +1 215 393 3000
www.alderfercompany.com

Freeman's
1808 Chestnut St, Philadelphia,
PA 19103
Tel: +1 610 563 9275/610 563 9453
www.freemansauction.com

Pook & Pook, Inc.
P O Box 268, Downington,
PA 19335-0268
Tel: +1 610 269 0695/610 269 4040
www.pookandpook.com

GUSTAVIAN DEALERS

Rupert Cavendish
610 Kings Road, London
SW6 2DX, UK
Tel: +44 (0)207 731704
www.gustavian-furniture.co.uk
info@rupertcavendish.co.uk

Rosemary Conquest
27 Camden Passage, Islington,
London N1 8EA, UK
Tel: +44 (0)207 3590616
rosemary@rosemaryconquest.com

Cupboards And Roses
296 Main Street, PO Box 426,
Sheffield, MA 01257, USA
Tel: +1 413 229 3070
armoires@earthlink.net

Julia Foster
84 York Street, London W1H 1QS, UK
Tel: +44 (0)7973 1466610
brbf@aol.com

Christopher Jones
Flore House, The Avenue, Flore,
Northamptonshire NN7 4LZ, UK
Tel: +44 (0)1327 342165
florehouse@msn.com
www.christopherjonesantiques.com

Eleish Van Breems Antiques
487 Main Street, Woodbury,
CT06798, USA
Tel: +1 203 263 7030
www.evbantiques.com
Swedish@evbantiques.com

US DEALERS IN AMERICANA AND FOLK ART

Thomas and Julia Barringer
26 South Main Street, Stockton,
NJ 08559
Tel: +1 609 397 4474
tandjb@voicenet.com

Bucks County Antique Center
Route 202, Lahaska, PA 18931
Tel: +1 215 794 9180

J M Flanigan American Antiques
1607 Park Avenue, Baltimore,
MD 21217
Tel: +1 800 280 9308
jmf745i@aol.com

Frank Gaglio, Inc.
56 Market St., Suite B, Rhinebeck,
NY 12572
Tel: +1 845 876 0616

Pat and Rich Garthoeffner Antiques
122 East Main Street, Lititz, PA17543
Tel: +1 717 627 7998
patgarth@voicenet.com

Guthman Americana
Mailbox PO Box 392, Westport,
CT 06881
Tel: +1 203 259 9763

Allan Katz Americana
25 Old Still Road, Woodbridge,
CT06525
Tel: +1 203 393 9356
alkatze@concentric.net

Nathan Liverant and Son
168 South Main Street, PO Box 103,
Colchester, CT 06415
Tel: +1 860 537 2409
nliverantandson@biz.ctol.net

Judith and James Milne Inc.
506 East 74th Street, New York,
NY10021
Tel: +1 212 472 1481
milne@aol.com

Monkey Hill
6465 Route 202, New Hope, PA 18938
Tel: +1 215 862 0118
info@monkeyhillantiques.com

Olde Hope Antiques Inc.
PO Box 718, New Hope, PA 18938
Tel: +1 215 297 0200
www.oldehopeantiques.com

Pantry & Hearth
121 East 35th Street, New York,
NY 10016
Tel: +1 212 532 0535
gail.lettick@prodigy.net

Sharon Platt
1347 Rustic View, Manchester,
MO 63011
Tel: +1 636 227 5304
sharonplatt@postnet.com

Raccoon Creek Antiques
PO Box 457, 20 Main Street
Bridgeport, NJ 08014
Tel: +1 856 467 3197

J. B. Richardson
6 Partrick Lane, Westport, CT 06880
Tel: +1 203 226 0358

Marion Robertshaw Antiques
PO Box 435, Route 202, Lahaska,
PA 18931
Tel: +1 215 295 0648

Cheryl and Paul Scott
PO Box 835, 232 Bear Hill Road,
Hillsborough, NH 03244
Tel: +1 603 464 3617

The Splendid Peasant
Route 23 and Sheffield Road, PO Box
536, South Egremont, MA 01258
Tel: +1 413 528 5755
www.splendidpeasant.com

The Stradlings
1225 Park Avenue, New York,
NY 10028
Tel: +1 212 534 8135

Jeffrey Tillou Antiques
33 West Street & 7 East Street,
PO Box 1609, Litchfield, CT 06759
Tel: +1 860 567 9693
webmaster@tillouantiques.com

US DEALERS IN TRIBAL ART

Marcy Burns American Indian Arts
PO Box 181, Glenside, PA 19038
Tel: +1 215 576 1559
mbindianart@home.com

Elliot & Grace Snyder
PO Box 598, South Egremont,
MA 01258
Tel: +1 413 528 3581

20TH CENTURY DEALERS

Aero
Yrjonkatu 8, 00120 Helsinki, Finland
Tel: +358 9 680 2185
www.aerodesignfurniture.fi

Alfies Antique Market
London NW8, UK
Tel: +44 (0)20 7723 6066
More than 100 dealers.

**American and European
20th Century Art and Design**
895-1/2 Green Bay Road, Winnetka,
IL 60093, USA
Tel: +1 847 501 3084
arts220winn@aol.com

Paul Andrews Antiques
533 Kings Road, Chelsea, London
SW10 0TZ, UK
Tel: +44 (0)207 352 4584
www.paulandrewsantiques.com

Art Deco Collection.com
546 & 550 Grand Ave, Oakland,
CA 94610, USA
Tel: +1 510 465 1920
www.artdecocollection.com

Bent Ply
Unit B58, 13 Church Street,
London NW8 8DT, UK
Tel: +44 (0)208 346 1387
bruna@bentply.com

Berg Brothers
London W11, UK
Tel: +44 (0)20 7313 6590
Mostly French and Italian; viewing
by appointment.

Classic Modern
Manchester, UK
www.deco-world.com
sales@deco-world.com

**Daniel Donnelly, Classic Modern
Furniture & Custom Services**
520 N. Fayette St, Alexandria,
VA 22314, USA
Tel: +1 703 549 4672
www.danieldonnelly.com

De Parma
London SW11, UK
Tel: +44 (0)7976 280275
Viewing by appointment.

Deuxieme
London NW8, UK
Tel: +44 (0)20 7724 0738

Geoffrey Diner Gallery
1730 21st Street NW, Washington,
DC 20009, USA
Tel: +1 202 483 5005
mgd@dinergallery.com
www.dinergallery.com

Eat My Handbag Bitch
London E1, UK
Tel: +44 (0)20 7375 3100
www.eatmyhandbagbitch.co.uk
Italian, British, and Scandinavian.

Fandango
London N1, UK
Tel: +44 (0)20 7226 1777
www.fandango.uk.com
European.

Fears & Kahn
Nottingham Antiques Centre,
Nottingham, UK
Tel: +44 (0)115 981 8501
www.fearsandkahn.co.uk

Inside
6 Clapham High Street, London
SW4 7UT, UK
www.insideoriginals.com
Tel: +44 (0)207 622 5266

John Jesse Gallery
London W8, UK
Tel: +44 (0)20 7229 0312

Larocco Galleries, Inc.
1010 Central Avenue, Naples,
FL 34102, USA
Tel: +1 239 434 5678
www.laroccogalleries.com

Lin/Weinberg Gallery
84 Wooster Street, New York City,
NY 10012, USA
Tel: +1 212 219 3022

Luna
Nottingham, UK
Tel: +44 (0)115 9243267
luna-online.co.uk
Ceramics and lighting.

Sarah Meysey-Thompson
Woodbridge, Suffolk, UK
Tel: +44 (0)1394 382144

**Modern Times,
Twentieth Century Design**
1538 N. Milwaukee Avenue, Chicago,
IL 60622, USA
Tel: +1 773 772 8871

Moderne Gallery
111 Third Street, Philadelphia,
PA 19106, USA
Tel+1 215 923 8536
www.modernegallery.com

Alexander von Moltke
46 Bourne Street, Pimlico, London
SW1W 8JD, UK
Tel: +44 (0)207 730 9020
alexvonmoltke@btinternet.com

Oval Interiors
Manchester, UK
Tel: +44 (0)161 374 1974
ovalinteriors.com
Viewing by appointment.

Annette Puttnam
Petworth, West Sussex, UK
Tel: +44 (0)1798 343933
Limed oak furniture.

The Retro Gallery
3 Cornwall Street, Edinburgh
EH1 2EQ, UK
Tel: +44 (0)131 2288251
www.twentiethcenturyantiques.co.uk

Sieff
Tetbury, Gloucestershire, UK
Tel: +44 (0)1666 504477
sieff.co.uk
Contemporary accessories and antiques
from 18th to mid-20th centuries.

Source
Bath, UK
Tel: +44 (0)1225 469200
source-antiques.co.uk
1950s aluminium kitchens, plus
furniture and lighting.

Jonathan Swire
Lytham St Anne's, Lancashire, UK
Tel: +44 (0)1253 721576
jonathanswireantiques.co.uk
Mirrors and pickled furniture; viewing
by appointment.

Tom Tom
London WC2, UK
Tel: +44 (0)20 7240 7909
tomtomshop.co.uk

Two Zero C Applied Art
London SW8, UK
Tel: +44 (0)20 7720 2021
twozeroc.co.uk
Viewing by appointment.

Gordon Watson Ltd
50 Fulham Road, London
SW3 6HH, UK
Tel: +44 (0)207 589 3108
gordonwatson@btinternet.com

SPECIALIST PAINT FIRMS

Authentic Paints and Stains
274 Route 13, Brookline, NH, USA
Tel: +1 603 672 2424
www.countryculture.net

Bleus de Pastel de Lectoure
Ancienne Tannerie, Pont de Pile,
32700 Lectoure, France
Tel: +33 5 62 68 78 30
www.bleu-de-lectoure.com

Colonial Williamsburg paints
Available from Old Village paints.
See below for details.
www.old-village.com

Farrow and Ball
Uddens Trading Estate, Wimborne,
Dorset BH21 7NL, UK
Tel: +44 (0)1202 876141
www.farrow-ball.com

Farrow and Ball in USA
Tel: +1 845 369 4912
usasales@farrow-ball.com

Farrow & Ball (Canada)
1054 Yonge Street, Toronto,
Ontario, Canada
Tel: +1 416 920 0200
farrowball@bellnet.ca

Fired Earth PLC
Twyford Mill, Oxford Road, Adderbury,
Oxon OX17 3HP, UK
Tel: +44 (0)1295 814399
www.firedearth.com

The Old Fashioned Milk Paint Co., Inc.
436 Main Street, PO Box 222, Groton,
MA 01450-0222, USA
Tel : +1 978 448 6336
www.milkpaint.com

Old Village Paints
PO Box 1030, Fort Washington,
PA 19034-1030, USA
Tel: +1 610 238 9001
www.old-village.com

John Oliver Ltd
33 Pembridge Road, London
W11 3HG, UK
Tel: +44 (0)207 221 6466

The Original Milk Paint Co.
PO Box 1331, Sun Valley 7975,
South Africa
www.milkpaint.co.za

Papers and Paints Ltd
4 Park Walk, Chelsea, London, UK
Tel: +44 (0)207 352 8626
enquiries@papers-paints.co.uk

Pratt and Lambert Historic paints
www.janovic.com

Stulb's Old Village Paints
Shaker Workshops, PO Box 8001,
Ashburnham, MA 01430-8001, USA
Tel: +1 978 827 9900
www.shakerworkshops.com

FABRICS

Beaumont and Fletcher
261 Fulham Road, London
SW3 6HY, UK
Tel: +44 (0)20 7352 5594
www.beaumontandfletcher.com
Traditional weaves, printed cottons,
and linens.

Bennison Fabrics
16 Holbein Place, London
SW1 8NL, UK
Tel +44 (0)20 7730 8076

Fine Arts Building
232 East 59th Street, New York,
NY 10022, USA
Tel: +1 212 223 0373
Aged and faded florals, many based
on archive French fabrics from 18th
and 19th centuries.

John Boyd Textiles Ltd
Higher Flax Mills, Castle Cary,
Somerset BA7 7DY, UK
Tel: +44 (0)1963 350451
www.johnboydtextiles.co.uk
Handwoven traditional horsehair
fabric.

Braquenié at Pierre Frey
251-3 Fulham Road, London
SW3 6HY, UK
Tel: +44 (0)20 7376 5599

Pierre Frey Inc.
12 East 33rd Street, 8th Floor, New
York, NY 10016, USA
Tel: +1 212 213 3099
Braquenié is known for printed cottons
based on its archive of 18th- and 19th-
century French fabrics.

Brunschwig & Fils
C10 Chelsea Harbour Design, Chelsea
Harbour, London SW10 0XE, UK
Tel: +44 (0)20 7351 5797
www.brunschwig.com
Historic American fabrics and
wallpapers.

Chelsea Textiles
7 Walton Street, London
SW3 2JD, UK
Tel: +44 (0)20 7584 0111
and
232 East Street, 59th Street, New York,
NY 10011, USA
Tel: +1 212 758 0005
Traditional embroidered fabrics and
crewel work.

Colefax and Fowler
110 Fulham Road, London
SW3 6HU, UK
Tel: +44 (0)20 7244 7427
Traditional printed cottons, chintzes,
silks, and weaves.

The Gainsborough Silk Weaving Co. Ltd
Alexandra Road, Sudbury, Suffolk
CO10 6XH, UK
Tel: +44 (0)1787 372081
Range of traditional handwoven silks.

Kravet London
G17 Chelsea Harbour Design Centre,
London SW10 0XE, UK
Tel: +44 (0)7795 0110
American minimalist fabrics.

Lelièvre
1/19 Chelsea Harbour Design Centre,
London SW10 0XE, UK
Tel: +44 (0)7352 4798
www.lelievre-tissus.com
Silks and velvets.

Marvic Textiles
G/26 Chelsea Harbour Design Centre,
London SW10 0XE, UK
Tel: +44 (0)20 7352 3119

Marvic Textiles USA Ltd
30–10 41st Avenue, 2nd Floor, Long
Island City, New York, NY11101, USA
Tel: +1 718 472 9715
Silks, toiles, and linens.

Osborne and Little Inc.
304 King's Road, London SW3 5UH, UK
Tel: +44 (0)7352 1456
www.osbornenandlittle.com
and
70 Commerce Road, Stamford,
CT 06902, USA
Tel: +1 203 359 1500
Traditional printed cottons and weaves,
including Nina Campbell and Liberty.

Sanderson
Sanderson House, Oxford Road,
Denham UB9 4DX, UK
Tel: +44 (0)1895 830037
www.sanderson-uk.com
Traditional velvets and printed cottons,
including William Morris archive.

Scalamandré
G/4 Chelsea Harbour Design Centre,
Chelsea Harbour, London
SW10 0XE, UK
Tel: +44 (0)20 7795 0988
www.scalamandre.com
and
942 Third Avenue, New York,
NY 10022, USA
Tel: +1 212 980 3888
Traditional silks produced on original
looms.

Stuart Interiors
Barrington Court, Barrington,
Illminster, Somerset TA19 0NQ, UK
Tel: +44 (0)1460 240349
Traditional weaves based on early fabric
archive.

Timney Fowler
now Dereham & Culpepper
355 King's Street, London
W6 9NH, UK
Tel: +44 (0)20 8748 3010
www.timneyfowler.co.uk
Mainly black and white fabrics and
wallpapers based on classical
engravings.

Warner Fabrics
G/11 Chelsea Harbour Design Centre,
Chelsea Harbour, London
SW10 0XE, UK
Tel: +44 (0)20 7376 7578
Traditional printed cottons and
damasks.

Zoffany
G/9 Chelsea Harbour Design Centre,
Chelsea Harbour, London
SW10 0XE, UK
Tel: +44 (0)20 7349 0043
www.zoffany.com
Traditional printed cottons, silks, and
weaves based on extensive documentary
fabric archive.

INDEX

Picture Credits

All photographs by Simon Upton, with the exception of the following: pages 9 below right, 146 left, 158-159, 161 left and back endpapers by Nacasa & Partners; pages 164 below, 169 left, 170-171 by Fabrizio Bergamo.

Credits (by location)

A Regency villa in the South of England appears on page 64-65, 75 above left, below left & right, 77 below, 79, 80-81, 85 above; Peter Adler's house in London appears on page 87 above right; John Barman's apartment in New York appears on pages 5 right, 175 above left & below right, 176 centre & below, 178 above & below, 179, 180 right, 185, 189 right; Giogio & Mariangela Busnelli's (B&B Italia) house in Italy appears on pages 164 below, 169 left and 170-171, 188 right; David Carter's house in London appears on pages 4 left, 35 left, 51 below left, 53 above, 59 above left & right, 67 above right, 68 above & below, 75 above left, 83; Jeannette Chang's apartment in New York, designed by Sonja & John Caproni, appears on page 91 right, 94-95 below, 163 below right; Martine Colliander of White Sense's apartment in Stockholm, Sweden, appears on pages 4 above left, 125 below left, 126 below left, 129 below, 133 below right, 138 centre, 138-139, 141 above, 187 left; Michael Coorengel & Jean Pierre Calvagrac's apartment in Paris appears on page 31 above, 32 below, 42 centre & below, 47; Hank & Debi di Cintio's house in Stockport, New York, designed by Frank Faulkner, appears on pages 53 below, 54 above & below, 55 above, 62 above; Laurent Dombrowicz & Franck Delmarcelle (of Et Cetera)'s house in northern France appears on page 138 above & below; Frank Faulkner's Catskill, New York, home appears on pages 8 below right, 51 below left, 55 below left & right, 56 above left & right, 57 above, 60-61, 63, 186 right; A London apartment designed by Ushida Findlay appears on page 87 above left, 95; Peter Franck & Kathleen Triem's house in Ghent, New York, appears on pages 142-143, 150, 153, 156 below, 156-157, 157 below, 161 right; A house in France decorated by Yves Gastou appears on pages 163 above left & right, below left, 164 above, 165 below left, 166 above left, centre & below, 167, 168, 169 right, 170 above & below, 171 below, 173, 186 far right; Elena & Stephen Georgiadis's London house, designed by John Minshaw Designs Ltd, appears on page 6-7; Walter Gropius House, a property of the Society for the Preservation of New England Antiquities, appears on pages 10 below, above right & below left, 147 above, 148 above, 156 above, 157 above, 160 above right; Emma Hawkins's house in Edinburgh appears on page 78-79, 82, 84; A house in Water Mill, Long Island, designed by Naomi Leff & Associates, appears on page 99 below left, 103 below, 110, 112 above right & below,113, 116, 119 below, 121 above, 188 far left; Peter Hone's apartment in London appears on page 15 below left; Warner Johnson's house in Claverack, New York, appears on page 90 above, 104, 105 centre, 111 below, 112 above left; Marianne von Kantzow of Solgården's house in Stockholm appears on pages 17 above left, 20 above, 22-23, 24 centre, 24-25, 42 above, 186 left; Marianne von Kantzow's shop Solgården in Stockholm, www.solgarden.net, appears on pages 25, 26; Hanne Kjaerholm's house in Copenhagen, Denmark, appears on pages 143, 145 above left, 147 below, 149 above left, centre left & below left, 150-151, 152 above right, centre right & below, 154-155, 158, 160 below, 189 far left; Pamela Kline (of Traditions)'s home in Claverack, New York, appears on page 67 below right, 70 above & below, 125 above left & right, 128-129, 130-131, 132 above, 137; Johannes Larsen Museum, Kerteminde, Denmark, appears on page 67 below left, 71 above & below, 76, 77 above, 85 below, 126 below right, 187 far left & left; Jerry & Susan Lauren's apartment in New York appears on page 117 above; A house in London designed by Frédéric Méchiche appears on pages 8 above right, 12-13, 29 below, 30 below, 32 above, 33, 36 below left, 40 above, 45, 48-49; Frédéric Méchiche's apartment in Paris appears on pages 152 left, 183; Juan Pablo & Pilar Molyneux's home in New York appears on page 30 above, 34, 35 right, 37-39, 40 below right, 41, 67 above left, 68-69 & 69 above, 186 far right; Mary Mullane's house in Claverack, New York, appears on page 8 below right, 127, 130 above, 131 right, 133 below left; Svartä Manor/Mustio Manor, between Helsinki and Turku in Finland, appears on front endpapers and pages 2 below, 4 below, 8 above left, 15 above left, right & below right, 16, 17 above right & below, 18-19, 20 below, 21, 22 above & below, 24 above, 24 bottom, 186 far left; John Pawson's London house appears on pages 9 below right, 146 left, 158-159, 161 left, 189 far right and back endpapers; Emmanuel Renoird's house in Normandy, France, appears on pages 2-3, 9 above right, 175 above right & below left, 176 above, 176-177, 179 below, 180 left, 181, 182-183, 184 above & below, 189 left; Denise Seegal's apartment in New York, designed by Sonja & John Caproni, appears on pages 13, 29 above right, 31 below, 36 above left & below right, 40 below left, 44, 165 above & below right, 166 above left, 168-169, 172 left & right; Mark Smith's house in London appears on pages 5 left, 109 above & centre left, 119 above, 120; Heinrich Graf von Spreti's house in Germany appears on page 10 above, 43, 46-47, 91 above, centre & bottom left; Eric and Gloria Stewart's manor house in southwestern France appears on page 11, 72-73, 99 above left & below right, 100, 101, 102, 103 above, 106, 109, 111 above, 114, 115 above & centre, 117 below, 118 above, 121 below,122 below, 123 below, 187 right & far right; Jerry & Maxine Swartz's house in Germantown, New York, designed by Frank Faulkner, appears on pages 4 centre, 52 above & below, 56 below, 58 above, 59 below left & right, 61, 62 centre; Andrea Truglio's apartment in Rome appears on pages 29 above left, 51 above left & right, 57 below, 58 below, 62 bottom; Althea Wilson's house in London appears on page 65, 87 below left, 90 bottom, 92 above, 93 below, 94 above & below, 160 above left; Vicente Wolf's apartment in New York appears on page 87 below right, 93 above, 93 below left; Robert & Josyane Young's house in London appears on pages 125 below right, 129 above, 130 centre & below, 133 above, 134-135, 136, 136-137, 140, 141 below; Hubert Zandberg's apartment in London appears on page 92 below.

Every effort has been made to trace the copyright holders, architects and designers, and we apologise in advance for any unintentional omission and would be pleased to insert the appropriate acknowledgment in any subsequent edition.

Artist

Sabina Fay Braxton 5 rue Daguerre, 75014 Paris, France
Tel: +33 1 46 57 11 62 (work appears on page 35 right)

Shops, Showrooms and Galleries

Peter Adler 191 Sussex Gardens, London W2 2RH, UK
Tel: + 44 (0)20 7262 1775 (by appointment only)
Et Cetera 40 rue de Poitou, 75003 Paris, France
tel: +33 1 42 71 37 11
Hawkins & Hawkins 9 Atholl Crescent, Edinburgh EH3 8HA, UK
Tel: +44 (0)131 229 2828
Peter Hone 3 Fournier Street, Spitalfields, London E1 6QF, UK
Tel: + 44 (0)20 7375 2757
Thomas Kjaerholm Rungstedvej 86, 2960 Rungsted Kyst, Denmark
Tel: +45 45 76 56 56 www.kjaerholms.dk
Solgården, Karlavägen 58
Stockholm, Sweden 11449 Tel: +46 8 663 9360 www.solgarden.net
The Althea Wilson Gallery
43 Burnaby Street, London SW10 0PW, UK
Tel: +44 (0)20 7352 9394
Traditions by Pamela Kline
PO Box 416, Calverack, NY 12513, USA Tel: +1 518 851 3975
White Sense (Martine Collinader)
Holländargatan 27, Stockolm 113 59, Sweden
Tel: +46 70 717 5700 www.mezzoshowroom.com
Robert Young Antiques
68 Battersea Bridge Road, London SW11 3AG, UK
Tel: +44 (0)20 7228 7847 www.robertyoungantiques.com

Designers and Architects

John Barman Inc.
500 Park Avenue, Suite 21a, New York, NY 10022, USA
Tel: +1 212 838 9443 www.johnbarman.com
Caproni Associates Inc.
200 Central Park South, New York, NY 10019, USA
Tel: +1 212 977 4010
David Carter 109 Mile End Road, London E1 4UJ, UK
Tel: +44 (0)20 7790 0259 www.alacarter.com
Michael Coorengel & Jean Pierre Calvagrac Design
& Decoration 43 rue de L'Echiquier, 75010 Paris, France
Tel: +33 1 40 27 14 65 coorengel-calvagrac2@wanadoo.fr
F T Architecture & Interiors
Peter Franck & Kathleen Triem
59 Letter S Road, Ghent, NY 12075, USA
Tel: +1 518 392 3721 architecture@taconic.net
Frank Faulkner 8 Franklin Street, Catskill, NY 12414, USA
Tel: +1 518 943 9220
Galerie Yves Gastou 12 rue Bonaparte, 75006 Paris, France
Tel: +33 1 53 73 00 10 www.galerieyvesgastou.com

Molyneux Architectural Interiors & Decoration
29 East 69th Street, New York, NY 10021, USA
Tel: +1 212 628 0097 JP@molyneuxstudio.com
Naomi Leff & Associates
12 West 27th Street, Manhattan, New York, NY 10001, USA
Tel: +1 212 686 6300 www.naomileff.com
Frédéric Méchiche
14 rue Saint Croix de la Bretonnerie, 75004 Paris, France
Tel: +33 1 42 78 78 28
John Minshaw Designs Limited
17 Upper Wimpole Street, London W1G 6LU, UK
Tel: +44 (0)20 7486 5777 enquiries@johnminshawdesigns.com
John Pawson
Unit B, 70-78 York Way, London N1 9AG, UK
Tel: +44 (0)20 7837 2929 www.johnpawson.co.uk
Emmanuel Renoird
18 rue de Bourgogne, 75007 Paris, France
Tel: +33 1 45 56 99 24
Smith Creative
15 St George's Road, London W4 1AU, UK
Tel: +44 (0)20 8747 3909 info@smithcreative.net
Andrea Truglio
75 via del Corso, 00186 Rome, Italy Tel: +39 6 361 1836
Ushida Findlay
4 Rodney Street, London N1, UK Tel: +44 (0)20 7278 6800
Vicente Wolf
333 West 39th Street, 10th Floor, New York, NY 10018, USA
Tel: +1 212 465 0590
Hubert Zandberg Interiors Limited
UK Tel: +44 (0)20 8962 2776

Museums

Johannes Larsen Museum
Møllebakken 14, Kerteminde, Denmark
Tel: +45 65 32 1177 kert-mus@kert-mus.dk
Mustio Manor/Svartå Manor 10360 Mustio, Finland
Tel: +358 19 36 231 www.mustiolinna.fi
Society for the Preservation of New England Antiquities
Harrison Gray Otis House, 141 Cambridge Street, Boston,
MA 02114, USA
Tel: +1 617 542 7307 www.SPNEA.org

Acknowledgments

There are so many people who are involved in creating a book like this, and I want to say an enormous thank you to everyone who allowed us to photograph their wonderful homes. I would also like to thank my friend and publisher Jacqui Small for all our collaborations. I would like to thank Simon Upton for his inspirational photography and for being as enthusiastic as I am about interiors – both historic and modern. My editor Cathy Rubinstein and Managing Editor Vicki Vrint have been thoroughly professional, understanding, encouraging, and have made even last-minute caption writing fun (almost!). Maggie Town has surpassed even her high standards with the design. Jill Bace has been at her most inspirational contributing to the text. Nadine Bazar found some wonderful locations, as did my dear friends Gloria Stewart and Fayal Greene. Julie Brooke and Mark Hill gave their support as always, and I really could not work on these wonderful projects without the support and understanding of my husband John Wainwright and my children Cara, Kirsty, and Tom.